ADVENTURE
YOUR
LIFE

THE TRUE STORY OF A LIFE-THREATENING ACCIDENT TURNED INTO TRIUMPH

LUKE BARNETT

CONTENTS

DEDICATION

I dedicate this book to the greatest adventurer I have ever met: my dad, Pastor Tommy Barnett. Dad, for my entire life I have had a front-row seat to observe what a life full of adventure looks like. I have never met anyone who lives with more passion for life, zeal to please God and remarkable joy. Your life has been an illustrated sermon for me to watch and learn from. It has been said that some things are taught and some things are caught. I am so grateful that you are my dad. Just watching you live has allowed me to catch your spirit and your desire to be the very best I can be for our Lord. Thank you for showing us what a life of adventure looks like. You are my hero!

I also want to thank my younger brother Matthew. Although you are five years younger than me, you have inspired me by your faith. I watched you go to Los Angeles as a twenty-year-old kid with nothing, and look at what God has done through your life. You have always carried the spirit of adventure. Your dream of running seven marathons on seven consecutive days on seven different continents elevated my belief that I could conquer the eight-hundred-mile Arizona Trail. Matthew, I love you. I am so proud of you! Thank you for pushing me to Adventure My Life.

I want to thank my daughter, Annalee. It was your dream to hike the Arizona Trail. You believed we could conquer it, and we did! Thank you for allowing your old dad to tag along with you. Thank you for caring for me with love, expertise and faith at the greatest moment of tragedy of my life. Thank you for not quitting when you felt like giving up. Thank you for being bold and brave and relentless in determination to finish the course. You are my quiet little assassin, the girl that doesn't speak a whole lot because you don't need to speak a lot. Your heart, ambition, character, and guts do all the speaking for you. I love you so much. I'm so proud of you.

Lastly, I want to thank my incredible wife, Angel. I tell you this often, but there is no one quite like you. When God made you, He broke the mold. You amaze me by your character, work ethic, and care for others. After my accident you were not sure if your husband would ever be the same. You didn't know if you would have to push your husband in a wheelchair for the rest of his life. You didn't know what the future held, but you were unfazed. You were a rock. You never wavered. There was never a moment that I doubted your love, concern, and dedication to seeing me through. Angel, there is no one quite like you on Planet Earth. In the pages of this book, you often refer to my courage and grit, but you are the most selfless, courageous, gritty person I have ever known. I have watched God use you over these past four years to see an entire city transformed. Colorado City and the Short Creek Dream Center are rescuing young ladies from human trafficking, restoring families, and giving young women a dream to live for — and that has happened in large part because you cooperated with God by answering His call to adventure your life, being the hands and feet of Jesus to the forgotten people of Colorado City. I love you with all my heart, and I am so proud of you.

CHAPTER 1

I HATE HIKING

We were gathered in a nice restaurant in Las Vegas for what was supposed to be a joyous send-off. The next morning, my daughter, Annalee, and I would head into the wilderness for a fundraising journey like we had never known — eight hundred miles from the southern Utah state line to the border of Mexico — and we were doing it for a good cause: to support the amazing work at our Short Creek Dream Center in Colorado City.

Everyone knew the intense, forty-day hike would test our minds, our bodies, and our emotions. But for reasons I didn't understand, the people at the celebration dinner seemed somber and even sad. My wife, Angel, is not a crier. Rather, she's one of the most upbeat, optimistic, focused people I have ever met — and yet tears brimmed in her eyes as we talked. She blinked them away and wiped a quick hand across her eyes, but she couldn't hide her emotions. Nobody else could, either. Here Annalee and I were, getting our minds and hearts ready to embark on this incredibly difficult journey, and our supporters were falling apart! Truthfully, it made me mad.

"What's going on?" I asked Angel in a whisper. "Why is everyone looking so sour?"

"I just … I'm worried for you," she said.

"Worried? Things'll be fine," I said. "We've got a whole crew. Robert, our trail expert, is coming along. He's a total pro. Annalee and I are physically ready — we've trained for this. I don't understand all the tears."

Angel tried to smile, but my words didn't change her emotions. Others, like my dad, with his usual positive, upbeat spirit, tried their best to say encouraging words, and we appreciated every one of them. But gloom still pervaded the gathering, and I figured it was because the task seemed daunting to everyone there. For our part, Annalee and I felt ready. We had prepared for this. They say leadership is a lonely place to be, and this seemed like one of those times.

But there's a reason not everyone takes an eight-hundred-mile walk across the state of Arizona.

The Challenge

To roll the tape back a bit, there was a time when walking from Utah to Mexico was the last thing I wanted to do. I remember when Annalee came up to me in our house one day. "Dad," she said in her soft-spoken but settled way, "I can't find anyone to do the Arizona Trail with me, so I'm going to do it alone."

Inwardly, I groaned. *Whoa, that's a big statement,* I thought.

Annalee, then twenty years old, had that determined sound in her voice. She tends to be quiet and thoughtful, and I knew that if she was saying this to me now, she had made up her mind.

"Yeah?" I replied, trying to sound casual as I considered what to say.

"Yup," she said.

She had already told me about this forbidding trail. Famously rugged and remote, it zigged and zagged, ascended sharply and descended just as precipitously for all those miles, as if designed to wear out the human body. It was so tough that only two hundred people per year reached the end. Yes, there are longer trails in the U.S. — the 2,650-mile Pacific Crest Trail, the gently wandering Appalachian Trail — but nothing in North America compares to the Arizona Trail for sheer brutality.

I also knew that Annalee has the world's most voracious appetite for adventure. She can't stand being cooped up in the city for long without escaping into nature to feel the freedom. Even more, she loves the challenge of hiking into remote places with only the supplies on her back, surviving for a few days, then hiking out. It gives her a rush, the same way hitting an awesome shot down the fairway does for me.

Our two worlds — the golfing green and the great outdoors — were just about to collide.

I couldn't let my young daughter go out on such a long adventure alone, so I boldly gave her some fatherly direction:

"Annalee, you can't do the Arizona Trail by yourself. Your mother will do it with you."

"Ha ha," my daughter responded.

We both knew I couldn't joke it away, and I already felt somehow that her adventure would pull me in. Big dreams have a magnetic effect on me — and on my children, I've discovered. Annalee had been pondering the Trail for three years. It was on every version of her bucket list. She had studied it, read stories of people who finished it, even researched its origins and found that it was created by a high school teacher. Still, it never made sense to me why someone would voluntarily take a long walk in the hot, dusty desert, carrying a heavy backpack and ascending a combined 113,000 feet of elevation. No wonder Annalee hadn't been able to convince anyone to go with her.

Some of her friends had already suffered the thirty-two-mile hike to Havasupai Falls that Annalee had led them on a year or two before. They thought they were signing up for a simple car-camping expedition, and instead my fearless daughter led them on a day-long hike to an admittedly beautiful waterfall where they slept in the dirt and ate whatever they'd packed in. She thought she was giving her friends a great adventure, but she may have created some enemies after they lost their toenails.

Sounds like a lot of fun, doesn't it?

Even at home, Annalee's wild streak popped up regularly. When the Arizona State Fair came to town, there she was, getting hooked up to the bungee jump "ride" by traveling carnies. If that isn't bravery, I don't know what is. (Not to be shown up, Angel bungee-jumped at the Fair, too. I was the only sane one in the family that day.)

But eight hundred miles with little access to water, no access to good coffee or air conditioning, and every chance of coming nose-to-nose with wild animals? This seemed a step too far.

"Annalee, I'm concerned about you going alone," I said honestly. "Anything could happen, especially down there by the border of Mexico. I know you love the outdoors, but I'm not exactly thrilled to think of you out there by yourself for a month and a half."

She nodded, and I knew she had already considered this. I also knew she was an adventure-loving Barnett, through and through, and every bit as headstrong as my family is rumored to be.

"Well, I'm getting married next year, and I figure this is my last shot to do the Trail," she said simply. "If no one will go with me, I don't have another option."

I groaned to myself again. Why couldn't all my kids love modern conveniences and coffee shops as much as I do?

Recruiting Myself

To put it as plainly as I can, I hate hiking.

Yes, I have done a fair amount of hiking in my lifetime, mostly to keep in shape or to spend time with my kids and friends. But unlike my trail-loving child, hiking for me is something to dread. I'd much rather be on a basketball court taking jump shots, doing head fakes and driving toward the hoop. Better yet, put me on a golf course, whittling my score down on a beautiful, manicured landscape. That's what gets my energy going, not long walks in the cacti-filled wilderness.

But after talking with Annalee about it, my internal conversation was going full steam ahead. I had a lot more reasons not to do it than I did to go along.

I don't want to do the Arizona Trail, even with Annalee, I thought. *It's just not my world. I like urban adventures, not rural ones. This is too far outside my zone. Plus, it might be the most strenuous, difficult thing I've ever done.*

I've done plenty of what I consider to be risky things.

I clearly recall the big zip-line course my family coerced me into doing — the one where you climb hundreds of feet up to a metal platform, then trust your life to a metal line that carries you for a mile over the tops of very tall pine trees. I even did it while it was raining! Extra points for Dad on that one.

As a thirteen-year-old, I went parasailing in Puerto Vallarta, Mexico. Then there was the time not long ago when my staff thought it would be a good idea if I went skydiving — just to make a good sermon illustration. No skin off their backs right? So I went tandem skydiving for my birthday. I had to overcome what felt like every fear I'd ever had to get into that plane and jump out of it while it was airborne. When the parachute opened, nausea hit me hard, and for two hours after landing (safely) on the ground, I didn't want to move because of the discomfort. Good times.

Apart from a dislike of heights and long trails, I consider myself to be pretty athletic. I have played basketball and golf my whole life and never injured my knees the way some guys do. I played quarterback on our high school football team. I even played college baseball. Impact injuries have happened — I split my head open playing basketball, and have broken each of my ten fingers at some point along the way — but my body has been generally hardy. I had arrived at middle age doing pretty well, I thought.

Truthfully, when it came to the AZT, I was more afraid of the scenery — which included, according to guidebooks, not just mountain lions and bears but wild horses, deer, elk, and wild burros. I'm not sure any man is a match for an angry, untamed burro coming at him in a desert wash, fifty miles from the nearest latte.

PREACHING TO MYSELF

Yet I heard my own words from sermons past echoing back to me. I often chided my congregation for reflexively saying, "I could never do that" when a new opportunity came their way. Here I was now, saying, "I could never do that." That was a warning sign to me, because when you believe you can't do something, you're automatically out of alignment with the truth. Jesus said nothing is impossible with God — and that includes hiking eight hundred miles. I knew if I started saying, "I could never do that," it would get easier and easier to keep saying it, and I would sell myself short, cause my world to get smaller and smaller, and maybe miss some part of the great destiny God has planned for me.

We have all watched people concede defeat before trying, accept failure without even taking a shot, and shut down God's work in their lives before even stepping out and allowing Him to start. Psalm 15:1-2 (NCV) says, "Lord, who may enter your Holy Tent? Who may live on your holy mountain? Only those who are innocent and who do what is right. Such people speak the truth from their hearts." (NCV) Whenever we say to ourselves, "I could never do that," we are not speaking the truth from our hearts, because none of us is absolutely sure we can't do something — and, again, nothing is impossible with God.

"I can't" is never God's view of you.

An old song I heard while growing up came back to haunt me as I contemplated the AZT — "Standing on the Promises of Christ My King." Each of us stands on something in this life, and ultimately we stand on what we think is real. There are a lot of really bright people who only stand on what they can see, hear, or feel. But that's not faith.

I was determined to walk by faith — and even hike by faith, if needed.

SURVIVING MINISTRY ADVENTURES

Beyond physical adventures, God had sustained me in ministry adventures as well. Believe it or not, those often were more dangerous.

There was the crazy, control-freak board I had faced in a Midwestern church early in my ministry — the one that literally locked me out of the church building at one point. (That congregation later turned around, and we left it in a healthy state — but oh, man, what a journey.)

There was the time in 2011 when my dad had unexpected heart surgery and I stepped in to lead the church without a lot of build-up or planning for what was ahead. Little did we know that God was transitioning the church from my dad to me. In that "dangerous" time, I desperately sought a dream for the church's future, and God gave me specific, huge goals for the ministry. I tell about that amazing journey in another book, *The Dream-Centered Life*.

I then weathered challenges to the big vision God gave us. When I took the reins from my dad, our church had one big, beautiful campus. But God gave me a vision for the entire state of Arizona to hear the gospel. In my heart, I saw multiple campuses sprouting up all over Arizona, and I was brave enough to share my vision for a "Christian state" with our congregation.

Then one day I was sitting in a restaurant and heard one man say to another, "Can you believe the pastor of that church is talking about Arizona as a Christian state? Who does he think he is?"

I could only smile. The real question was, *Who do I think God is?* because no man can accomplish a dream that big with his own mind, strength, or talents. In the ten years after that, our ministry grew to ten campuses, a Christian school, two Dream Centers, and three pregnancy clinics to provide young women an alternative to abortion. I'm so glad I didn't limit the dream to what I could do, because only God could do what He did in just that first decade.

FAMILY OF ADVENTURERS

Another motivation to hit the trail with Annalee was our family legacy.

You see, I come from a family of adventurers and pioneers, going way back through the generations. Our family is ridiculously competitive in a (mostly) healthy way. We're a hard family to out-do, and we support each other in all the new, crazy things each of us cooks up.

For example, I watched my dad run from Phoenix to Los Angeles

(420 miles in twenty days) to raise money for the Los Angeles Dream Center in the 1990s — when he was in his sixties. Who do you know who has run that many miles from one major city to another across some of the hottest, most forbidding desert on the planet? That's my dad. His run inspired people from around the world to give money to buy the Queen of Angels Hospital, now called the Dream Center, in downtown Los Angeles. There are nearly three hundred Dream Centers around the world today, and it all began with a run across the desert. Wow.

My dad also wrote a book years ago called *Adventure Yourself.* It impacted my life, and I decided as a young man to adventure myself like he did whenever possible.

Recently, I watched my brother, Matthew, run seven marathons on seven continents on seven consecutive days. Only about forty people from around the world have attempted to do this, and Matthew can testify that it was crazy hard. My family always dreams up the impossible—then does it. That is fuel for me. In my heart I had always admired Matthew and my dad for accepting great challenges, and I secretly wished that somehow God would tailor a great adventure like that for me. I wanted foot knowledge, not just head knowledge.

The Barnett adventure legacy is broader than just my brother and our dad, though. Danielle Boatwright, my cousin, won the *Survivor* competition in an early season of the reality show, and recently competed in a reunion of past winners. My own wife, Angel, competed nationally in hunt-seat equitation — more popularly known as show jumping — and was ranked sixth in the nation for driving a buggy! What a woman.

On the ministry side, we Barnetts are known for preaching that life is an adventure — that you need to keep an adventurous attitude toward whatever you do and that you are called to be a person who says, "Yes."

I myself have preached numerous sermons on the subject, like the one called "Dying to Live." In that sermon, I told people there are death predictors online. You put your height, weight, and health factors into a form and it tells you when you can expect to die! How horrible.

On the platform that Sunday, I had one of my associate pastors sit on what I call "the most dangerous object in your house": the easy chair. I dumped Doritos and cookies on his belly, put a remote control in his hand, and the congregation serenaded him to sleep. It was gross! Yet that's an accurate picture of how many of us live behind closed doors. I told people that an adventurous life is within their grasp, and sometimes it takes using a crowbar to pry yourself out of "normal."

I don't think my family is alone in our calling to be adventurers. God's plan has always been for humanity to be visionaries and dreamers. It's our destiny. Only blind people have no vision; some may have had one but lost it along the way.

I often wonder how history will judge this generation of Americans. Around the world, the gospel is exploding in places like China, Africa, India, and South America. We hear reports of tremendous revivals. So why is it that in the West, the Church is filled with so many bored, uninspired people? They show up on weekends out of obligation, but there is really no enthusiasm or vision behind their participation. Maybe that is one of the reasons we are not seeing God move with more definitive power in the United States — Americans don't have an appetite or vision for it. In fact, maybe we have a vision for something else!

Today in America, we are exposed to more advertising in one year than a person who lived fifty years ago saw in an entire lifetime. By some estimates, we see three thousand ads every single day, all designed to create discontentment and make us think our lives are not good enough — that we are missing out on a bunch of stuff that will make us feel better. These ads shape our minds, whether we want them to or not. They cause us to pursue someone else's desires and dreams rather than having our own.

I once read a book called *Culture Jam: The Uncooling of America*. The author wrote,

> Life in America is like life in a cult. We've been recruited into behaviors and patterns that we did not consciously choose. Dreams, by definition, are supposed to be unique and imaginative, yet the bulk of our population is dreaming the same dream. It is a dream of wealth, power, fame, plenty of sex and exciting recreational opportunities. When the entire culture is dreaming the same thing, imagination has been taken captive. An alternative dream requires animation by a different narrative. (Kalle Lasn, Morrow/HarperCollins; Nov. 1, 1999)

The culture around us has indeed captivated our dreams so that even Christians are dreaming of the same things that people outside the Church dream of. It is the dream of gaining wealth and fame, having plenty of sex and exciting recreational activities. But if you read the description of the early Church in Acts, you'll see it was built around two kinds of people. Acts 2:17 reads,

"… in the last days," saith God, "I will pour out of my
Spirit upon all flesh: and your sons and your daughters
shall prophesy, and your young men shall see visions,
and your old men shall dream dreams." (KJV)

When God birthed His Church, He declared it would be filled with
visionaries and dreamers, people whose minds are animated with visions
and dreams from heaven so they live different lives and pursue grander
visions. That's you and me!

One time, Angel and I visited the Colosseum in Rome. I stood there,
looking at this architectural marvel, imagining what it must have been
like when it was filled with fifty thousand people cheering, "Maximus,
Maximus!" Do you know what they were cheering for? Gladiator games
in which people savagely murdered one another. Why were they killing
one another? Was it over land rights or legal disputes? No, it was for
entertainment. The crowd would watch these murders, then go home
and eat dinner. During four months of one caesar's rule, ten thousand
gladiators died. That's how little the Romans valued life.

Many Christians, too, were martyred on the very ground on which I
stood — until one day a Christian monk named Telemachus was visiting
Rome for the first time and heard a roar coming from the Colosseum.
He sat in the stands among the thousands of other people. Everyone was
cheering and celebrating as someone was killed, but Telemachus was so
grieved by what he saw that he got up, walked to the front, and jumped
into the arena amongst the gladiators.

"In the name of Christ, stop!" he yelled.

The gladiators paused — and then they killed him in front of those
fifty thousand people. But for the first time in anyone's memory, silence

fell in that arena of death. Then one person left, then another, until the entire place emptied out in silence. That event was the catalyst that inspired Emperor Constantine I to outlaw the gladiator games — all because one Christian visionary, one dreamer, looked at the culture and said, "There has got to be another way." He gave his life for that dream.

Telemachus wasn't the only one to do such things. The early Church was marked by such visionaries and dreamers. In Alvin Schmidt's book *How Christianity Changed the World* (Zondervan, 2004), he writes about the impact these early believers had on history.

> Numerous institutions were started by the followers of Jesus Christ. Hospitals first originated in the 4th century under Christian influence. Institutions for the blind, the deaf, and for the mentally ill are some other institutions started by Christians. The Red Cross is still another major institution that came about as a result of Christian influence. The profession of nursing is another one.

In the eighteenth and nineteenth centuries, the fight against the slave trade was led by Christians William Wilberforce in Britain and William Garrison in the U.S. On it goes — Christians are born again to be visionaries and dreamers!

Earlier in the history of the Church, James, the brother of Jesus, wrote, "Religion that God our Father accepts as pure and faultless is this: to look after orphans and widows in their distress" (James1:27, NIV). Most Christians are familiar with that verse, but what you may not know is that when James penned those words, caring for orphans and widows was a revolutionary idea. At that time, widows and orphans were typically sold as slaves (and often trafficked for sex). Society disdained them so much that no one even cared what was happening to them — until a band of visionaries and dreamers came along to declare that, "Religion that God our Father accepts as pure and faultless is to look after orphans and widows in their distress." What all those early Christians had in common is that God set their minds free and gave them a vision that was animated by heaven so they would no longer settle for the same fleeting goals their culture accepted.

Now I had an adventure staring me in the face, challenging me to literally walk out my own advice. Talk about a message hitting home! In a way, I was going through what I recognized as a "call narrative." These are the steps people take when setting out on an adventure. Often, a call is rejected at first. The called one insists, "I'm not worthy" or "I'm not able." Peter, one of the disciples of Jesus, did this. So did Gideon, who became a great warrior but began as a cowering kid.

In response to our "No" and our excuses for not stepping out in faith, God always gives a promise. To Peter it was, "I will make you a fisher of men." To Gideon, it was the fact that God already saw him as a mighty warrior.

Most called people try to procrastinate, but procrastinating is a sneaky, subtle way of saying "No" to God's call on your life. Procrastinating feels allowable because it's not phrased as open defiance, but it amounts to disobedience all the same. In fact, there is a quite scary statement in the Bible: "Anyone who knows the right thing to do, but does not do it, is sinning" (James 4:17, NCV).

Was going on the AZT the right thing to do? I wasn't completely sure, but I knew procrastinating wasn't a viable long-term strategy. Eventually, you reach a point of decision.

The more I thought about a long hike, the more I saw that challenges are my bread and butter — once I get over the initial butterflies.

I don't want to go on a massive hike, but if I put my mind to it and really dig in, I know I could pull it off, I thought.

Fresh Vision

Like most people, I often focus more on what I want to get done than who I want to become. That's a common trap people fall into. The truth is, I want to become the kind of person who takes on new challenges. I don't just want to get through my daily to-do list. I want to be someone different — someone better — because of my choices. This requires intentionality. I have done this in the past with financial goals, fitness goals, family goals, and "follower" goals as a Christian.

Psalm 90:12 says, "Teach us to count our days aright, that we may gain a heart of wisdom" (NABRE). Life is precious and pretty short, but with proper effort we can "gain a heart of wisdom." That's remarkable. Yet every day, people come to their final day — sometimes without knowing it — and realize they have thrown away their one and only life for no good purpose.

Such people live a life of perishing day by day. It's a visionless life, and the Bible warns, "Without a vision, people perish." That doesn't mean people keel over and die right there. It happens over years, or decades. Shoulders slump, eyes dull, days feel long, and nights feel restless. Perishing happens right in the midst of living. Your life looks normal to those around you, but something is dying inside you — and you know it.

I went through such a season before my dad had that unexpected heart surgery. I was between ministry assignments and felt burned out. The dreams had leaked out of my heart. In previous seasons, I had been bursting with fresh vision and revelation, but at that time I needed a fresh infusion. I was "perishing" for lack of a vision.

I never wanted to experience that feeling again.

BITING THE BULLET

As I thought about all of this, my instinct for adventure — and my protective fatherly impulse — finally overcame my self-protection strategy. I realized that Annalee was going to do the hike no matter what. Someone had better do it with her, and it looked like that someone was me.

Goodbye, easy chair. Goodbye, comfortable routine. Goodbye, air conditioning. Goodbye, lattes.

In their place, I started to imagine the benefits of hiking with Annalee. A vision must be vivid to maintain my motivation. I've always thought of vision as a picture of the future that creates passion in you. I sit with God and imagine what He has for me in the next project, trip, sermon, or endeavor of any kind. His creativity flows into my thoughts, and my activities gain an eternal purpose. Napoleon Bonaparte said, "Imagination rules the world." Einstein said, "Imagination is more important than knowledge." Imagination is a gift from God that only humans have. God uses our imaginations to build the future through our faith. That's why Paul commanded us to, "Let heaven fill your thoughts; don't spend your time worrying about things down here" (Colossians 3:2, TLB).

In other words, let your imagination be the place where God supplies heaven-sent visions for what's next in your life. Never base your dream on what you think you could do; base your dream on what you think *God* could do.

I was certainly imagining spending a lot of time with my

almost-married daughter. A hike like this would allow me to plunge into her world and see things through her eyes for a while. She was always noticing sunsets and flowers, things that easily escape my attention, and now we could enjoy those things together. I also imagined myself hearing from God in a fresh, supernatural way. I liked the idea of putting myself in a situation where He might "whisper" to me about the future of my family, church, and more.

I would also catch up to my brother and dad, so to speak, by setting a new bar for Barnett adventures. No one had attempted an eight-hundred-mile hike across an entire state before. And who knew? Maybe I would come out more physically fit than I had ever been.

"Annalee, I'll do the hike with you," I told her one day. She glowed and nodded. "When's a good time to go?" I asked.

"Usually early fall, like September or October," she said. "That way there's still water flowing, and we avoid the heat."

"Let's do it," I said.

"Let's do it," she replied with a huge grin.

I was committed.

CHAPTER 2

TRAINING FOR THE ADVENTURE OF A LIFETIME

We set a start date of September 24, 2020 — eight months away. As the year developed and the world plunged into an entirely different season of challenges — i.e., the COVID-19 pandemic — our plan of hiking in remote wildernesses seemed even more well-timed. Everything would be closed and locked down, anyway. Why not hike from Utah to the border of Mexico?

As I assessed my current hiking condition, it occurred to me that the only overnight experiences I'd had in the Arizona desert were catered ones in pretty cushy circumstances. For example, I had been invited to go on an all-expenses paid, six-night, seven-day whitewater rafting trip down the Grand Canyon as part of a men's leadership event a few years earlier. Thirty guys in four or five boats paddled through rapids — or held on for dear life — as our guides taught us to dig in with our paddles and pull hard through the rough stuff. Some rapids were so lofty that rafts went airborne, landing with a big splash on the other side of a peak. Not only that, but the water, released from the bottom of the dam at Lake Powell, was 47 degrees Fahrenheit. If you tumbled in, swimming was barely an option because hypothermia would soon set in.

We steered our rafts to shore and got out to hike in canyons and crevices. We beheld massive waterfalls and pools, even climbing down cliffs where one wrong move would have meant a fall of seventy-five feet. Then it was back into the raft for more paddling.

But it was not the primitive experience you might imagine. The trip was outfitted by a company that laid out amazing catered meals every night. They did all the grunt work so we could have guy time and not worry about it. The hardest part was hiking out nine miles on the Bright Angel trail, each of us carrying a thirty-pound backpack. I trained hard for that hike — and I killed it, beating everyone in our group by an hour. Angel and our girls picked me up at the big resort at the top, and I felt invincible.

With that in mind, once I chose to do the AZT, I felt confident I could rise to the challenge. Annalee and I started training the very next day, hiking at least four miles a day, even when it was 112 degrees out. Soon, we were up to eight or ten miles a day, at least five days a week. We started carrying two gallons of water with us, not to drink, but to get us accustomed to the weight. Each gallon weighs around eight pounds, and we would be carrying more than that in the form of tents, sleeping bags, flashlights, and also water at times. The vibe was good. Heading out for training became something we looked forward to.

Then one day, I was hiking a rugged trail called Elephant Mountain Trail in Cave Creek. It was June, and by the end of the eight-mile hike, my body was depleted and dehydrated by triple-digit temps. I had used up all my water. I looked around for help, but I was alone. Other hikers were too smart to be on the trail in heat that intense. As I made the final turn down the homestretch, my left calf and hamstring locked up with cramps. I fell to the ground and rolled around in the dirt in agony. My left leg was unusable, paralyzed with pain, and there was no one to help me. After ten minutes or so, I summoned my energies, got my body up, and limped to the car. Disaster had been narrowly averted.

Another time, I was on the same trail, losing daylight, so I decided to run the final two miles. Bad idea. Dim visibility led me to faceplant on the trail. I scraped much of the skin off one side of my face as well as my left shoulder. When Sunday rolled around, people at church asked if I had been in an MMA fight because of the bruises on my face. I said, "No, this is what happens when you back-talk Angel." Those incidents gave me a lot more respect for the adventure we had chosen.

At home, I began watching videos of experienced hikers who had started the AZT but were unable to complete it. They either got injured or the extreme exposure forced them to quit prematurely. In some cases, their bodies simply couldn't handle the rigors of such a long, up-and-down hike. One career hiker documented his AZT adventure with daily videos. After fourteen days, his hiking partner's iliotibial (IT) band wore out and he had to quit. I didn't even know what an IT band was. What I did know was that these people were experienced hikers, with a great love and passion for it, yet they couldn't complete the very thing Annalee and I — a couple of city folk, by comparison — were attempting to do.

The more I watched them, the more I realized I lacked a key element they possessed: passion and the drive to finish. They — and Annalee — were motivated simply to complete such an epic hike. They were excited by the thought of it. I wasn't as much. My hope was more or less to be able to say I'd done a big thing. That wasn't enough. It would be difficult to accomplish something this large without a deeper, driving motivation. I needed some fuel, some cause that would inspire me with each step. I needed a passion to keep me in the race when I grew tired and doubts and fears crept in to weaken my resolve.

Strong motivation inspires you to rise above your abilities and perform at a peak level. I would need that — even more than I knew.

A Big Dream Requires a Cause

"I have to tell you," I admitted to Annalee one day, "I don't have the passion needed to accomplish the AZT. But I think I know where to get it."

"Where?" she asked as we walked home from one of our training hikes.

"A great cause," I said. "We should hike this trail for an eternal purpose."

She nodded. She knew a good idea when she heard one. She probably also knew it would keep my head in the game.

We didn't have to look far for our great cause. Our church had been on a miraculous journey with the people of a once-troubled little town on the state line between Utah and Arizona. Colorado City, a remote place by design, was the hub of the Fundamentalist Latter-Day Saints (FLDS) group led by Warren Jeffs, who is now serving a life sentence for child sex abuse. This polygamist offshoot of the Mormon religion is a network of families committed to secrecy, separation, child brides, and doctrines even the rest of the Mormons reject. The sect in Colorado City numbers around ten thousand people, and counts thousands more in other communities around the U.S.

When Jeffs and his followers were prosecuted for crimes against minors, their leaders and the members of their "preferred" families fled the town — leaving behind many "lesser" wives and children. These helpless people had virtually no idea how to support themselves or relate to the outside world. Many of the girls — now mothers — had been given in marriage in their early teens to much older men. The only world they knew existed behind the closed doors and walls that protected their homes and compounds from scrutiny. These "protections" also kept them ignorant of how to live any other way.

Under Jeffs's reign of fear, secrecy, and control, men didn't even lead their own families. They performed construction jobs, gave the money to the FLDS, and received food based on measures of obedience. At any given time, their families could be taken from them, so some dubbed them "Velcro families." Everything was based on punishment. Women were considered property and couldn't think for themselves. Fear of losing one's family was always present. If a husband or wife disobeyed, all the children or even the spouses could be reassigned to other families. Many of the kids didn't even know who their real mothers were. There was no sense of individual identity. Birth certificates weren't kept.

After Jeffs was incarcerated in 2011, a couple from San Diego, Jena and Glyn Jones, felt called to make Colorado City their ministry base. They had been criss-crossing the U.S. in their RV to help Samaritan's Purse and other organizations with disaster relief. The credibility they established in Colorado City helped connect them to one of Jeffs's former wives, Brielle Decker. As Jeffs's sixty-fifth wife, she had been awarded his former house in a settlement by a judge who oversaw the former leader's properties. One day, Brielle invited the Joneses on a tour of the forty-five-bedroom house and related her dream of turning it into a place of healing and refuge for women and children coming out of the FLDS.

The Joneses had the same thought: *This would be a great Dream Center.*

Brian Steele, director of the Phoenix Dream Center (PDC), had already become involved with the city of Short Creek, Utah, when the marshal's office there raided homes, and needed a refuge where he could send teenagers pulled out of abusive situations. PDC volunteered.

One girl came in a prairie dress. She had been a "gift bride," one of the young adolescents given to older men as wives. Through the Joneses, Brian, who serves on the Arizona governor's council for human trafficking, learned of Brielle's dream for the former Jeffs property. The Phoenix Dream Center purchased the twenty-nine-thousand-square-foot home and several other buildings with a vision to make that dream come true.

But the task ahead was daunting. Angel visited there and later recounted that the spiritual heaviness emanating from the compound was palpable within the city limits. "We walked into the house and could feel this oppression," she said.

We realized that polygamy is a version of human trafficking because the girls are born into it and traded like property. The populace of the Short Creek community Jeffs and his "elite" members abandoned in favor of secret compounds in other states and countries was 72 percent under the age of seventeen. Most were not educated beyond a fourth-grade level and had no job skills.

They were also traumatized from the abuse and confusion inherent in their former religion, and from being left behind by the leaders of their community.

Our teams began remodeling Jeffs's former house to turn it into a community center. With the help of churches and Christian groups from across the nation, they transformed the forty-five bedrooms, giving each a unique and uplifting theme: beach, horses, garden, camping, and so on. They also created a library, chapel, game room, large open areas for potluck dinners and other gatherings, an art therapy corner, and a sensory room for kids with autism, ADHD, and anxiety.

The Short Creek Dream Center (SCDC) began hosting regular basketball games, game nights, after-school tutoring sessions, and community events that drew hundreds. People would walk through the door feel uplifted for reasons they didn't even know. Healing, slowly, had begun.

Soon, more than sixty women were receiving regular counseling at the house, along with crisis housing, vocational training, help putting together resumes, job placement services, and trauma-informed family counseling. Much of our team's work was helping people process what had happened to them, as well as getting them birth certificates and food. The SCDC fully adopted my dad's ministry motto of "Find a need and fill it, find a hurt and heal it" — words which adorn our teams' vehicles and T-shirts. Joyce Meyer gave substantially to support the new ministry in an ongoing way. Her impact on it was huge, and we couldn't have done what we did there without her help. We also owed a big "thank you" to Glyn and Jena for helping that Dream Center get started. God used them in a significant way there.

Because there is no grocery store in the Short Creek area, the need for food was critical. Dream City Church raised $400,000 to buy a building that we used for food distribution, and with the help of the Convoy of Hope and a Phoenix-area food bank, the SCDC began feeding four thousand people a month from an eleven-thousand-square-foot warehouse which receives weekly donations via semi-truck trailers. Teams also deliver boxes of food directly to homes. Convoy of Hope also helped secure 3,500 pairs of shoes and socks from major clothing brands to donate to children in town, many of whom didn't own shoes and therefore could not attend school.

School administrators called in tears to thank our leaders.

Still, we had to be careful not to be perceived as using the former Jeffs properties the way Jeffs did — to command spiritual allegiance. We made the food bank facility a non-threatening place of community interaction and engagement. We had to recalibrate the residents' way of thinking and let them start dreaming of a new future.

Today, we feed 60 percent of the town every week. The entire house that once belonged to Jeffs is now filled with women in residential recovery and restoration processes. Angel recently visited the city with Utah's attorney general. Former Arizona Attorney General Mark Brnovich also made a trip to Colorado City, as did gubernatorial candidate Kari Lake. In 2018, Megyn Kelly did a five-minute documentary on the Short Creek Dream Center's efforts to help revive and rescue a whole town. The nation was paying attention to the transformation.

Brielle is now a member of our Short Creek Dream Center staff. Interestingly, our staff is mostly made up of minorities, which is a change in a town that was previously only white.

GENEROSITY-DRIVEN

Helping the SCDC became my driving cause for hiking the AZT. I wanted to be generous — and I wanted to lead others in generosity as well. If the AZT were just about me and Annalee walking a long way for some kind of personal triumph, that would not satisfy me. But knowing that lives were on the line gave us great motivation. As usual, I find that plugging generosity into any endeavor adds a hundred times more energy and meaning to it. Even family vacations or business ventures ramp up when you make generosity part of the basic plan.

I like to say that you will never be remembered for what you spend on yourself. You will only be remembered for what you spend on others. After all, it all belongs to God, anyway. Think of how easy it is to give away other people's stuff — then see your own stuff as God's! Give it away freely.

I encourage generosity because I see amazing things happen when people become generous. Proverbs 11:25 says, "A generous person will prosper; whoever refreshes others will be refreshed" (NIV). God promises that generous people will be replenished and cared for throughout their lifetimes. In Mark 10:29–30, Jesus said,

> "I can guarantee this truth: Anyone who gave up his home, brothers, sisters, mother, father, children, or fields because of me and the Good News will certainly receive a hundred times as much here in this life. They will certainly receive homes, brothers, sisters, mothers, children and fields, along with persecutions. But in the world to come they will receive eternal life." (GW)

No stock broker can guarantee those kinds of returns on any investment, let alone for eternity. They may offer an ROI — return on investment — but they cannot offer an EROI — eternal return on investment. Only God & Son, Inc., can do that, and I like to say they've been doing business with people like you and me for two thousand years.

With that goal in mind, our trip took on a whole new aspect. I was using what I had — all my abilities that would go into a hike and a fundraising campaign — for something I loved. Annalee and I set a big target: to raise $1 million from supporters and sponsors of our hike. I shared the idea with our team at the church and they sprang into action, creating a plan with all the moving parts needed to accomplish that God-sized goal. Key donors were contacted, and a series of events planned to get people on board at any level of support.

Now I felt the rush of momentum behind me. This wasn't just a private hike anymore. There was a lot on the line — especially for the girls at the Short Creek Dream Center who would benefit the most.

CHAPTER 3

HITTING THE TRAIL

As our team planned and prepped the fundraising campaign for the Short Creek Dream Center, Annalee and I kept training and getting mentally prepared for what we were about to tackle. But as the day grew closer, our AZT planning team sensed I was still nervous about the practical aspects of the hike. I was leading a megachurch with eight campuses. I was overseeing two Dream Centers with nearly four hundred residents. I was overseeing a staff of nearly three hundred people. I didn't have time to become an expert at navigating the trail and surviving in the wilderness without getting lost, or in using all the equipment we would need. So in the interest of safety, the team contacted an amazing man named Robert Owens. He took me and Annalee through a few different training seminars on navigation, medical emergencies, and so on.

Robert is a former Navy SEAL medic who was voted the fittest man over the age of sixty by a popular men's fitness magazine. Our team asked him to hike the first stretch with us to help us get familiar with all the equipment — tents, gas stove, and so on. He agreed, and I was greatly relieved. My confidence in being able to finish went up.

I also felt challenged by Annalee's faith. She was simply fearless about the AZT.

If that little rascal believes she can do it, then I'm going to stir up my faith and believe I can, too, I told myself.

LAUNCH WEEK

Finally, our launch day was just a week away. Annalee and I had put in approximately fifty miles of training each week for thirty-two weeks. That's approximately 1,600 miles of hiking — just to get ready for the AZT! Now it was time for the rubber of our hiking boots to hit the trail.

To involve our supporters in what we were doing, we planned a big event we called "Night of a Million Dreams." It was for the many people and churches from far and wide that had committed to support the Short Creek Dream Center. Pastors and supporters from all over America met us in Las Vegas, which is the closest major airport to Colorado City. That night, our family and a few close friends went to a local steakhouse to celebrate Angel's birthday, just six days away, and to say goodbye to Annalee and me.

The night was supposed to be joyous, but as I mentioned earlier, it had an unexpectedly somber flavor. It wasn't just sentimentality over saying goodbye to us for a few weeks. The people's expressions went into actual sadness, which I didn't quite understand. Some shed tears. We all knew the risks involved in doing the AZT, but I still wanted to say, "Come on, people, cheer up! We are not going to die. Send us off with some faith and hope." But the evening continued to feel ominous.

The next day, thirty pastors, supporters, and their spouses boarded a bus with us for the two-hour drive to Colorado City. On the way, we watched documentaries about this obscure little town and tried to explain the horrors of what Colorado City had been to the women and children living there. But nothing could really convey those truths like actually being there. Stunned looks and ashen faces appeared as these men and women toured Warren Jeffs's former mansion, where women were essentially kept in slavery. They were shocked that a place like this existed in the USA.

That night we held our first city-wide outreach for Colorado City. We held a big barbecue and concert in a beautiful park situated against the red rock mountains that have made that area famous. Colorado City sits right near Zion National Park, known for its orange-and-red cliffs. That night was a major breakthrough for our Dream Center. Three thousand people — a third of the town — showed up to see what we were about and to enjoy free food and music. It was a huge blessing to them. At the conclusion of the concert, I stood up and invited people to follow Jesus. This was the first time in the history of the city that the pure gospel had been presented. Dozens responded to the call for salvation. What a night it was!

The Dream Center had already been supplying tons of nutritious food to the town every month for some time. Most of the families were abandoned by their husbands, who fled the area with their other wives, leaving behind the most vulnerable women and children. These single-mother families were in dire need of basic items, which we arranged to provide via regular deliveries. In addition to the all the services to the single mothers and their children that I detailed in chapter 2, we also provided residential counseling and rehabilitation for women and men who had been sexually abused in an environment where that was considered normal. In the very place where they had lived in captivity, we now offered freedom through the power and love of Jesus Christ.

The event was also a big win for our pastors and supporters, who saw clearly what we were doing and the impact their support would make.

On the bus ride back to Las Vegas, my dad stood before the guests and asked them to partner with us in seeing Colorado City transformed. I remember Keith Craft, pastor of Elevate Life Church in Frisco, Texas, standing to his feet to say, "Our church will give the first $100,000 if the other churches will match it." His seed gift opened the door for a flood of generosity. Those pastors joined together to help finance the work. Commitments were nearing $1 million by the time we got back to Las Vegas. Annalee and I sat there and watched all of this happen, and it inspired us even more to get out on the trail the next day to do our part.

That night, we and our team drove to a little town near the AZT trailhead in Utah called Kanab and checked into our hotel room. But instead of having a free night to chill out before the big day, I got a call from Robert Owens. Like the SEAL commander he once had been, he ordered me to join him in the lobby to go over our equipment. To be honest, I was relying on Annalee and our team to cover me in this area, at least for the first few days as I familiarized myself with the gear. It sounds naïve to me now, but I prefer to stick to my areas of strength and let others lead where they are strong. But Robert was waiting in the hotel lobby to walk me through every detail of my backpack — tent, sleeping bag, flashlight, headlamp, miniature gas stove, and about fifty other pieces of equipment, all laid out before us. Step by step, he trained me how to use them all. We were there for nearly three hours, and though I pretended to be retaining it all, I felt completely overwhelmed.

Still, it didn't bother me. I knew things would work out okay. Our team was strong.

INTO THE WILD

At 5 a.m. on September 24, we got out of bed and drove to the trailhead with our team of seven guys, along with a group of staff from the Short Creek Dream Center. It was all very exciting. The chill air promised a fresh new adventure. Before us were views and natural beauty that seemed to have been taken directly out of a painting. My heart rose with good feelings, but when I looked over at Angel, I noticed she was crying again.

What is with her? She never cries, I thought. As she kissed us goodbye, silent tears coursed down her cheeks. Many others saying goodbye at the trailhead were teary as well. I was in such high spirits that I dismissed it as a normal reaction in a moment of separation. With cheers from our team, Annalee, Robert, and I took the first steps of our odyssey and left the rest of the team behind.

The first day passed without incident as the desert forest engulfed us. Gone were cell phones, traffic noise, and most of the sights and sounds of modern life. In their place were the *swish-swish* of our hiking shorts, the creaking of straps on our backpacks, and friendly conversation as we traveled together for the first time as a team of three. After a while, my pack didn't seem as heavy. My steps found their rhythm.

I can do this, I thought. *One step at a time.*

Sometimes you move forward, knowing you will get power along the way. People often complain that they don't see God moving in their lives. But you don't get the power until you go on the journey. When Jesus did His first miracle of turning water into wine, He instructed the servants at the wedding He was attending to fill six large containers with water. I can only imagine them saying to one another, "Why? We don't need water, we need wine!" But they did as Jesus commanded, and somewhere between the point of the servants filling the containers with water and the guests tasting it, Perrier became chardonnay. Power was released along the way.

Another time, when some lepers asked Jesus to heal them, He first told them to go show themselves to the high priest. The high priest served as an unofficial health department in ancient Israel. He would confirm any healing that took place. Again, I can imagine one of the lepers saying, "Why should we go to the high priest to have him tell us what we already know, that we are lepers and we are dying?" But maybe another leper said, "Guys, what do we have to lose? Besides, Jesus has that look in His eye that something might happen along the way." And the text says that while they were on their way to see the high priest, they were cleansed. They received power along the way.

I was receiving power along the way, too, but still, by hours six and seven, my feet were saying something different. Blisters were popping up like bubbles on a cheese pizza. I kept moving, but by late in the day, when I took a break to rest, I could hardly get going again.

I thought practice hiking would toughen up my feet, I thought somewhat disappointedly. Apparently, it hadn't been enough.

Our destination for the night, part of the Kaibab National Forest, had recently burned in a wildfire. The sky darkened as we prepared to pitch our tents, but nothing could have been darker than the blackened landscape around us. Soot was everywhere, and I couldn't help but think, *My first time really camping outdoors, and everything's covered in ash!* Everything turned black — our camping gear, our hands, our feet, and our faces. It was miserable. Annalee's trail journal from that day read in part:

> *Super emotional start, super nervous. Worried about weight of bags but as we started hiking things fell into place! Kept seeing these cute horned lizards. They were so tiny. Need to find water tomorrow. Having fun, but tired and very sooty.*

As I lay in my tent after dinner, my feet whined at me about every one of the twenty miles we had just covered. I quietly thought, *I am so worn out right now, it's impossible for me to get up and do this again tomorrow.*

But when we woke up at 6 a.m., after twelve hours of sleep, I was amazed by how good I felt. Still stiff, but I was very impressed by how quickly the body recovers with good rest. I was ready to go.

The rhythm of walking returned. The sounds were more familiar now. I was growing fond of the peace of nature, the calls of birds I hadn't heard before, the scent and feel of nature up close.

Three-quarters of the way through day two, Robert came up next to me and said, "I've texted ahead, and want to have the crew pick me up at the next stop. I'm slowing you down. You guys know how to do this. You're doing wonderfully. I'm strong, but I'm not as fast as you."

Extreme fitness in one area doesn't mean you'll be a fast hiker able to endure really long days, he said. Hiking uses a specific set of skills. Annalee was pressing the pace, and I was trying competitively to keep up with her — which might have explained the blisters. Near our next campsite was a road, and our crew met Robert in a truck. With some last-minute tips for taking care of my feet, he waved goodbye and Annalee and I struck out on our own, hiking another fourteen miles to camp.

That night, I was worn out again, but hoped that my body would bounce back overnight. And it did. A routine was being established. I was even comfortable with most of the equipment by then. Annalee wrote in her journal:

> *Got up at 6 AM and was in a good mood, body felt restored, got some coffee and a Pop-Tart in me. Took us about an hour and a half to pack up camp and then we were off. We*

went through a series of intense elevation changes, which really wore us out. Dad didn't want to stop for a break because he was worried he wouldn't get back up, so I made him eat a Snickers while I snacked on peanut M&Ms. Had plenty of water, didn't drink much. Could see the Grand Canyon and Humboldt from where we were, AMAZING views. Tiring but awesome day. Dad's feet were/are jacked up.

GLAMPING

Part of our strategy for making it the whole way was having some nights where we met up with our team. Certain parts of the trail were accessible to campers. On those nights, Annalee and I got the blissful opportunity to take real showers, hang out with the team, eat a hearty meal, and sleep in actual beds. A member of our church, Ken Moss, generously had bought us a new camper with a kitchen, living room, bedroom, and shower in it for this very trip. I had never appreciated teamwork more! To know that on certain nights we would relax in a comfortable environment with our team was a huge boost on long days.

By this time, I felt very much in stride. We were making great time. I reflected on a message I had preached called, "The Weight Will Make You Great." It talks about the weight of preparation versus the weight of burden. Jesus doesn't want us to carry weights of burden, but the weight of preparation will draw more out of us. It will make us stronger, better, and greater. None of us can expect to fulfill a massive destiny if we only want to carry little five-pound weights. In the same way, while at first a five-pound backpack seemed heavy to me, now a pack weighing twenty-five pounds hardly bothered me. Annalee even wrote of me, "Dad seemed to be feeling good today, I had trouble keeping up with him on the downs." *Yeah, take that, Annalee!*

On day five we reached the north rim of the Grand Canyon. Our original, preferred plan was to hike down twelve or thirteen miles, camp in the canyon that night, and hike the remaining thirteen miles to the south rim the next day. But we couldn't find a spot to camp in because an influx of hikers was coming off the Pacific Crest Trail due to wildfires. They jumped on the AZT instead and took all the camping spaces. Also, most campsites weren't available at the time due to COVID restrictions, so the only option was to do all twenty-six miles in one day, rim to rim — way down, then way back up and out.

For once, I was probably more excited than Annalee was. She hates going downhill and loves going uphill. I am the opposite. I excel at going downhill and feel like a bona fide sprinter. But going uphill exhausts me more quickly. Going uphill, she's sneaky fast, but going downhill hurts her hips and knees. As we stepped onto the rim trail and began to descend, I felt mischievous sense of glee as I set the pace. For days I had been telling Annalee, "You're going too fast. I can't keep up." I also reminded her, "When I was your age, I could bury you on this trail, but now I can't." Now it was payback time — time to see if the twenty-year-old could keep up with the fifty-one-year-old heading down the steep decline. I didn't plan to make it easy on her.

While I effortlessly burned down the hill, my mind was free to reflect on our big cause. I thought of Luke and Konstance Merideth, executive directors of the SCDC. Both had come from really broken pasts and were living portraits of recovery that families in Colorado City could look up to.

Luke had been raised in perpetual poverty by a heavily addicted mother who died from complications of drug use when Luke was nine-teen. Seeking structure, he joined the military and was a combat medic with the U.S. Marine Corps for five years. Survivor's guilt haunted him after his service in Iraq, and once out of the military, he turned to drugs for relief. God was a foreign concept to him at the time. As a nurse, he began diverting medications and became hooked on heroin and methamphetamines.

The drugs were merciless. By age twenty-six, Luke had had three heart attacks. He also was convicted of stealing medications. Finally, he went to the Phoenix Dream Center for help. I like how he put it: "They ministered to my potential, not my problems."

This amazingly talented guy gave his life to Jesus and then came on staff with Brian. He served as the vehicle fleet manager, then became the executive project administrator working with capital improvements — finding new buildings and ensuring the quality of our operations. He also earned his business degree from Grand Canyon University, and then a master's degree in substance abuse counseling.

He met Konstance, who also came to the PDC to recover from addiction. As coworkers in Colorado City, they fell in love and were soon married. Konstance is the perfect combination of class and fearlessness. In Phoenix, as a residential assistant (a "house mom," basically) at our residential program for sex trafficking victims, she would go onto the streets at 2 a.m., walk up to prostitutes, and tell them they are loved and that the Dream Center had options for them to enter a recovery program. Sometimes the women jumped into our van immediately. Often, they took a number and called when it was safe to do so.

Konstance was later promoted to chief programs officer. Then she and Luke took on the challenge of leading the SCDC. Today, SCDC gives away 70,000 to 100,000 pounds of food every month. Luke and Konstance both coach sports teams at a local high school — he for wrestling and she for volleyball. The ministry also offers counseling free of charge to anyone in the community. Innovative approaches include equine therapy, art and music therapy, and horticultural therapy in a greenhouse where people grow their own plants. The center employs strategies from the PDC such as cognitive behavioral therapy and family systems therapy — helping people figure out healthy roles in their family environments. This helps them make sense of relationships within complex and large families like the ones in the AFLDS, where one person might have forty cousins, multiple mothers, and dozens of siblings and half-siblings.

The Meridiths find that religion can still be a sore topic for some of the people they serve. Some profess to never want to hear about spiritual things again. Some parents quit giving their kids any moral guidance at all, having been burned by moral instruction themselves. Others take the view of, "That wasn't God. We need a real God in our lives." The SCDC uses a "good Samaritan" model, helping anyone with any faith and creed, while being unashamedly Christian in its approach. Our teams even teach morals and boundaries in local public schools.

One high school gave our team a list of what kids wanted for Christmas, and the SCDC spent thousands supplying those gifts. When Luke and Konstance asked what schools needed most on an ongoing basis, administrators said they wanted a neutral place for tutoring because a sixteen-year-old boy coming out of a closed religion probably only has a third-grade education. Integrating him into public schools is difficult.

Such children need help to catch up with their peers, so the SCDC turned a room of the former Jeffs compound into a learning center with a couple dozen computers.

As I bounded down the Grand Canyon, I thought of all God had done since we took on that project with no financing and little knowledge about Mormon culture, let alone this particular subculture. We hadn't known if the people in the town would accept us or see us as a controlling religious entity. It would have been hard to blame them for not trusting anybody; they had been so abused and burned by their former leaders. And yet now, our team was seeing truly amazing results day after day.

I'm happy to be able to say that our ministries such as StreetLight, Where Hope Lives, the Phoenix Dream Center, and the SCDC form the nation's largest human sex trafficking rescue operation. Our combined programs offer more rooms and more beds than any other organization, and the kicker is we have 92 percent success rate for recovery. No recovery organization in America comes close to that.

These thoughts filled my mind as I left Annalee in the dust on the way down to the Grand Canyon floor. We weren't just strolling through God's most beautiful landscapes. We were raising lots of support for young women the world had treated like trash — and who God was rescuing like treasures. As for the sights around us, Annalee journaled later:

Trail got very beautiful, weaving in and out of canyons, over footbridges, through streams, etc. Crossed the Colorado River and it was breathtaking.

Then the pain began.

PASSING THE STONE

Unfortunately, I am well-acquainted with the feeling of passing kidney stones, as it has happened to me several times. Before the hike, I went to the Cooper Clinic in Dallas, Texas, to get a full medical check-up. Cooper Clinic is like the Mayo Clinic on steroids — an amazing place to get a complete physical. The staff informed me that I had three stones lodged in my left kidney that might (or might not) ever be jarred loose. "Just be aware they are there," they told me. Now, that familiar pain surprised me as we crossed the low plateau and headed up to the canyon's south rim. Within a mile or two, the discomfort became incapacitating. I sat down, then leaned back as the pain grew worse. I could go no further.

"I don't know how I'm going to make it out," I gasped to Annalee.

"I think I have a little bit of signal. Let me call Mom," she said, examining her cell phone.

At the top of the canyon, Angel and the team were waiting for us. Our plan was to sleep in a hotel when we came out of the Grand Canyon, since we had gone five straight days in the wilderness and needed a break. Up top, Angel had some of her famous and extraordinarily effective supplements for moments such as these. The question was how to get them to me so far down in the canyon?

Thankfully, the answer was at hand in the form of Annalee's fiancé, Kaden, a young man of many abilities. While I labored in pain on a rock below, Angel assigned him to run down the pathway to me and deliver the rejuvenating drink. He finally arrived where I lay in agony. I don't know what was in Angel's potion, but it was powerful. I got right back up and continued the ascent. Kaden and Annalee prayed for me as well, and the pain from the kidney stone went way. It had obviously passed through my ureter into my bladder. Prayer works, and so do Angel's potions.

At the rim, I hugged Angel and thanked her for her miracle water. I still felt weak and fragile enough to go to a local clinic, and they pumped fluid into me intravenously for several hours to rehydrate me. Sure enough, that night I saw the devilish little kidney stone come out. It was blessedly out of my body — and good riddance.

But I was about to go through an even bigger learning curve when Annalee and I got separated from each other … and lost.

CHAPTER 4

A BLOW-UP
IN HIGH COUNTRY

The next leg of the hike was beautiful. We had finally reached the high country near Flagstaff, and passing before us were the most beautiful elk, followed later by forty or more wild horses rumbling over the hillside. Annalee wrote: "Put my music in and cruised, miles flew by. Didn't see much more wildlife or hikers."

In Flagstaff, a lovely mountain city that sits more than seven thousand feet above sea level, we stayed a couple of nights in a hotel, sleeping in real beds and eating normal food. Olympic athletes and marathoners come to Flagstaff to train because of the high elevation. Refreshed, we then traveled through lake regions alive with huge elk, grand pine trees, and massive mountains. It was awe-inspiring to be out there with just my daughter and a vast view of God's magnificent creation.

The next day Annalee wrote:

Dad likes to go fast in the morning. First ~ 10 miles were mostly downhill with some quick inclines that were annoying. Feet were kind of bothering me. Took a break at 5 miles

and Dad did a devotional. Started up again and I put in
some music and started cruising. We accidentally spooked
a herd of wild horses and they went running and bucking.
There was a massive white one, so beautiful.

We were approaching the dreaded Mazatzal Mountains, a really rough three- or four-day section where we would be out of contact with our team in a remote region. Pitched elevation gains made carrying a lot of water impractical. Streams had dried up because it was a drought year. Fires recently had also raged throughout the state. In many places where flowing water was normally found, the washes were bone-dry. The only other places to find and filter water were in stagnant ponds, or maybe a cow trough with mucus and who-knows-what-else in it. We would take our bottles, dip them in, and hope the filters worked really, really well.

Our plan in that area was to rely on the assistance of a nearby rancher who owned horses and mules, and who was friends with some cowboys in our church. We would carry our first day's water, and on day two, this rancher and his wife would ride in on horses and supply us with more. They were one part of the big team working to make it all happen. We were thankful for them.

But before then, we had a series of beautiful days. Annalee wrote:

Woke up well rested and like I'd slept like a rock. Hair was
crazy lol. Got dressed, ate a bagel, drank coffee, and hit the
road. Had a long bumpy ride to drop off. Cold this morn-
ing. Dropped off in a pretty woodsy area. Nice walking for
first 4.5 miles and then we came out onto a plateau with

not a lot of trees. Saw a big herd of cows and came close to a bunch of cute calves. Took a break at 5.5 miles and ate my honey bun. Started up again and walking on the trail was awful. Every step was an ankle twister, there was no shade, and for some reason my hip started to ache. Only one good view of upper Lake Mary. Tried to ignore the pain but I was kind of miserable. Pushed through it till lunch and stopped for a sandwich and Doritos. Hit the spot. Left us at 12 miles down and only 8 to go. Next 4.5 mile were still nasty and without shade. Took a break. Chilled and ate a Reese's in the shade. Felt a lot better and only had 4.5 to go. Nice shade, trees, and good walking. Body felt good and I was really setting a good pace. Ignored the hip and all of the sudden my right calf spasms. Stopped, waited a couple of seconds, and decided to walk it off while Dad took the lead. A mile from pickup Dad announces he's got a shin splint. Made it to the end tired, beat up, and dirty, but we made it. Good day, gonna be even better tomorrow.

Yet the next stretch of the trail was where things seemed to go haywire for everyone.

SEPARATE WAYS

It began with an ugly incident between me and Annalee. I was really fatigued, and my legs had started to wear out badly. Merciless elevation changes plus rocky, uneven terrain took a constant toll. I hadn't slept well. My margin of grace was really thin.

The same was true for Annalee. She wrote:

> *Starting the Mazatzal Mountains today. They're infamous for being the most rugged, remote, and harsh mountain range of the trail. Woke up at 4:30 a.m. Prayed and took off. Stripped jacket pretty quick because the first 4.5 miles were straight uphill. Very difficult.*

The Mazatzals have low visibility and confusing trails, and Annalee continued to outpace me. This worried me because at divides in the trail, we could easily become separated. She had an app on her phone that helped her navigate these forks in the road, and at the time I didn't know I also had it on my phone, so I was relying on her to keep us together.

"These trails can get confusing," I told her early in the day. "When we come to these T's, please wait there for me."

But the trail was full of elevation gain — four thousand feet, to be exact — and that got her motor going. She took off like the wind, leaving me behind to slog up what she had just breezed over.

I admire Annalee's quiet drive. I call her "the silent assassin" because her disposition is reserved, but she has an internal motivation like few I've ever known. I saw it in action when she ran cross country in junior high and played golf in high school and college. Both sports require plenty of internal discipline, and she excelled in them at a young age.

Being with her on this trip was the most meaningful thing to me, personally. She would soon be married and out of our house. This was a once-in-a-lifetime growing opportunity for both of us. We would have something no one else in our family had.

The only problem was, her drive was now pushing her beyond where

I could see or hear her. It wasn't long before that creeping fear of being lost came over me. I stopped to try to hear her footsteps on the trail ahead. Nothing. I pressed on and crested the high point of our elevation that day. I strained my eyes to look over the vast desert forest, and still I saw no sign of her.

"Annaleeeee!" I yelled as loudly as I could. No response. I yelled her name again and again. "Annaleeeee!"

Did a mountain lion get her? I wondered. *Did a bear get her? Did she fall and can't respond to me? Where is she?*

I kept screaming her name, totally panicked and at a loss over what to do. I had a gun with me. *Maybe I should fire it off,* I thought.

Finally, the thought came: *Use the app.* I suddenly remembered that I had the same trail-navigation app she did, only I had not used it. I pulled out my phone, somehow got a signal, registered with the app and found my location. Following its instructions, I navigated my way down the mountain and found Annalee sitting there, cool as a December day, waiting for me as if nothing had happened.

By this time, we had been on the trail eighteen days, and with all the wear and tear and long hours, I was at my wits' end. I tore into my daughter with words.

"You think you're so cool leaving an old man behind," I sneered. "You're twenty years old — of course you can go faster. But if you don't want to hike with me, just go ahead without me. I don't want to see you the rest of the day. I've got the app. I'll manage just fine. Now get out of here!"

Tears appeared in her eyes as I railed at her.

"No, Dad, I'm sorry. I don't want to," she said, but I was spitting mad.

"I don't want to see you right now," I said. "Get out of my sight!"

It was by far the most severe conversation I'd ever had with her, and it wasn't right for me to say what I did. I was worn out. I felt no control over my tongue. I knew people made bad decisions when depleted. I had even preached a message titled, "What to Do When You've Run Out" about how nobody makes good decisions when they're worn out. Yet here I was, breaking all fathering rules and making a really bad decision of my own.

Obediently, but with a hurting heart, Annalee pulled on her backpack and headed down the trail without me. She was crying as she went, and I sat there calming down and trying to regain some focus for what this day might become. My reserve tanks were empty. Nothing — not rest, not food — seemed to draw up the needed energy.

Galatians 5:16–17 says something very important that I was clearly neglecting:

> But I say, walk by the Spirit and you will not carry out the desire of the flesh. For the flesh sets its desire against the Spirit, and the Spirit against the flesh; for these are in opposition to one another, so that you may not do the things that you please. (NASB1995)

The flesh is the desire to please yourself as opposed to pleasing God. We all battle with the flesh, and I was battling it now. By contrast, walking in the Spirit means moving through life in step with the Spirit. The Apostle Paul didn't say we would never have the desire to walk according to our own selfish impulses. Rather, he said we wouldn't "*carry out* the desire of the flesh*.*" This means the Spirit is powerful enough to override fleshly desires — if we let Him.

I had discovered that walking in the Spirit feels like no longer having to force things. The Bible calls the Spirit "a wind." It pushes and empowers you in the right direction. It's like being on a moving sidewalk at an airport. When you step on the moving sidewalk, you can still walk, but now you're gliding as you do. You're getting to your destination quicker with less wear and tear. Something underneath you is propelling you along.

As I walked alone after yelling at Annalee, I certainly didn't feel the Spirit propelling my bad attitude. Rather, I felt Him pushing me back to His way. When I am out of step with the Spirit, it feels to me like He is saying, "Come over here and be with Me, Luke. I'm not going to bless what you're walking in. Fall in line with Me and we'll be together." That's an amazing offer to me — that God desires to spend time with us. He is our temple, our house of God, our dwelling place. Jesus even promised before He ascended to Heaven, "And be sure of this: I am with you always, even to the end of the age" (Matthew 28:20, NLT). Whether or not you feel it or believe it, God just wants to be with you.

In the very last book of the Bible, it even says, "God's dwelling is with humanity, and He will live with them. They will be His people, and God Himself will be with them and be their God" (Revelation 21:3, HCSB). That's what life is about. My part is to learn to continually focus my attention on God. You can almost boil the practice of spiritual life down to one single statement from Scripture: Psalm 16:8 (ESV) reads, "I have set the Lord always before me." Have you ever considered doing that? If we forget and start looking for peace and fulfillment elsewhere, we just come back and set Him before us again. That's the way I want to live my life.

When I do that, God's characteristics actually become my own.

When you abide in Christ, He rubs off on you! Like being in the rain will make you wet, and the hot sun will make you sweat, being in His presence will fill you with peace, love, patience, gentleness, and so many good things.

I needed His presence badly at that moment because walking in the flesh had me feeling like I was slogging through a spiritual graveyard. I didn't feel His blessing on my upset thoughts. Something had to change, and I knew it had to be me.

LOST

Out of sight on the trail ahead of me, Annalee was so discombob-ulated by my outburst that she hit a fork in the trail and went right, even though the app said to go left. A little while later, I came upon the same divide, but I somehow got it right by following the app. I kept hiking, thinking I was half a mile or so behind her, when in fact she was going farther down the other trail. At some point, she realized she had made a wrong turn and came back to the T, but I was already past it. She waited more than thirty minutes for me to pass by, thinking I hadn't arrived there yet.

Where is Dad? He must be lost in the wilderness, she thought, while I was actually ahead of her. So Annalee decided to backtrack to try to find me. After a mile or so she concluded that I was lost in the vast desert forest, and she worried that I had tripped and hit my head, been bitten by a snake, or something worse.

She pulled out her phone to try to get a signal and call me. Her phone didn't work at that point on the trail, and after waiting for me she decided the best thing to do was to run ahead as fast as she could to try to finish the fifteen remaining miles for the day. At that point she could consult with the cowboy and his wife, who were delivering water to the drop-off spot, about a rescue plan and get a helicopter to come back and help me. She strapped her pack on and engaged her famous speed to eat up the miles that lay between her and civilization. As she did, she kept checking the dirt for traces of my shoeprints.

But I thought Annalee was ahead of me so I was hiking faster and faster. After five miles or so, I finally stopped to eat a peanut butter and jelly sandwich. I hadn't seen a glimpse of Annalee since I sent her off in anger, and I was more than a little worried about the state of things. *Is she far ahead of me? Where will I find her?* Eating would help me think clearly, so I sat on the rim of a canyon, overlooking the vast valley below me.

I seriously blew it as a dad, I chastised myself. *I know I was worn out, but I shouldn't act like that. I don't respond that way normally. What is the matter with me? Oh, God, please help me make this whole thing right.*

That's the moment I saw my daughter coming up the trail behind me, tears coursing down her cheeks. I looked at her; she looked at me and said, "Thank You, Jesus," and I got up and we ran toward each other. We hit in a hug, and I wrapped my arms around my little girl.

"I'm so sorry, Annalee," I said.

"I'm so sorry, Dad," she replied, muffled into my shoulder.

She cried and so did I on the side of that mountain. Relief surged over me as I gripped her. "Thank You, Jesus. Thank You, Jesus," we both kept saying.

It was the only time we got mad at each other on the trail. I made it right. We apologized again and again to each other, saying how stupidly we had behaved — especially me, because I was older and knew better.

Together we sat on that bluff, drinking in the view of that beautiful valley, made more beautiful by the presence of each other.

"I really thought you were lost," she said. Then she laughed: "I thought I had killed you. It was one of the scariest moments of my life."

"For once, I took the correct turn and you didn't," I said.

It didn't matter anymore. We were back together as a team.

CHAPTER 5

A CREATURE IN THE NIGHT

The rest of that day continued to be rough. My body and mind were wearing down, the big blowup had depleted us further, and we were far from finished with the hard hiking. Annalee could tell I was struggling as the sun sank to the horizon. I was sweating like crazy and losing a lot of salt. I kept on eating salt to try to replenish it, but it didn't seem to work. I was cramping up like I had in the Grand Canyon, and Annalee was worried I would pass another stone.

When I hit walls like that, I draw on past wisdom and even preach to myself a little bit. It's a way of goading myself on, inspiring my mind. My dad often talks about feeling he can go higher. Even at the great milestones of his life, there's always a little man (imaginary, of course) who shows up and urges him on to greater things. For example, when my dad pastored a church in Davenport, Iowa, in the 1970s, he brought Johnny Cash to town for an evangelistic event, the biggest thing to happen there in ages. At end of that Billy Graham-style crusade, the "little man" showed up and said, "What happened here was amazing, but you can do more."

When Dad built the biggest church auditorium in Phoenix, the little man said, "This is a great peak, but you can do more." When Dad cofounded the Dream Center with my brother Matthew, the little man said, "There is yet more." The point is, to succeed in life you have to keep going the extra mile, take the extra step, and get yourself into miracle territory.

My blistered and bruised body was certainly in miracle territory right then.

The Spirit of Resilience

Some call it resilience, the ability to endure, bounce back, keep going, and achieve more. Plenty of studies have been done on people who went through deep trauma: survivors of prison camps, people who experienced brainwashing or were in traumatic accidents. Many experienced a loss of hope, a nagging sense of resignation, isolation, and defeat. However, others who faced those same traumatic situations found that a fierce spirit rose up inside them. They refused to give up, and they looked for creative solutions and ways to take action. If one thing didn't work, they looked for another.

These people say to themselves what World War II concentration camp survivor Victor Frankl said: "No matter what my captors might take away from me, they cannot take away my freedom to choose my own attitude." People with that kind of resilient spirit actually enlarge their capacity to handle problems. They become stronger and learn to look forward to challenges in life. They become greater through pressure.

One young lady in Colorado City who had been forced to stay in the FLDS sect when leaders fled called our team unexpectedly and asked someone to rescue her from the religion. Her daughters, ages thirteen and fourteen, were coming up for arranged marriage, she said, and she didn't want them consigned to a life of slavery. She also had a biological son she had kept in hiding. The SCDC rescued that family, and later Joyce Meyer interviewed one of the girls on her show. Theirs became a story of hope.

To believe you can escape such a traumatic situation takes resilience. I admired that young lady as I plodded along. She embodied Proverbs 24:16, which says, "the righteous falls seven times and rises again." By contrast, "the wicked stumble in times of calamity" (ESV). She had been victimized her entire life, and yet she held onto hope that something good could come of it. She took responsibility for her hope. Whether or not she knew it, she was doing what Paul said to do when he wrote, "... one thing *I do*: forgetting what *lies* behind and reaching forward to what *lies* ahead, I press on toward the goal for the prize of the upward call of God in Christ Jesus" (Philippians 3:13-14, NASB1995).

Even our physical bodies speak of this forward orientation God expects us to take. Our eyes are on the front of our heads, not the back. Our ears are shaped to hear what's happening ahead of us more than what's behind. Our arms and legs face forward so we can reach into the future and walk toward the next opportunity. In fact, only one part of our bodies faces the wrong side, and when you think about its function, maybe through that God is saying, "There is just some stuff you need to leave behind."

At the moment, I was the one falling behind.

"Dad, I'm concerned you're not going to make it to camp," Annalee said. "You're taking such little steps and we're not making much progress. Plus, you look bad."

She was right. Cramps were seizing my legs and calves especially, and my face was contorted in a continual wince. The supplements Angel had packed for me weren't helping anymore. My condition was worsening, and we were late making it to the agreed-upon meeting and camping spot with the cow-couple, Travis and Allison. In fact, they had to ride further than they had intended to find us. We were very grateful. If they had simply dropped the water off at the campsite, we might have been in real trouble if we couldn't find it. But they didn't stay to chat with us long.

"We're going to turn around and try to make it out of here," they said. We thanked them as they rode off to have their own adventure.

Meanwhile, Annalee and I got our tents out. She wrote,

> *Set up camp in a wonderful spot facing the setting sun. I ate an MRE Breakfast Skillet and Dad ate Indian curry (both were good). Had a cup of coffee and some Oreos and got into my tent with the sun down. Read a portion of an old book before falling asleep. One of the most dramatic days to date on the trail.*

On my mind was the bear poop we had seen along the trail all day. I could picture a bear thinking how fortunate it was to have two delicious meals wander into such an out-of-the-way place. Annalee and I both had little handguns to scare mountain lions off. We hadn't needed them until now, but I made sure mine was right next to me as I tried to fall asleep on my tiny little air mattress.

One of the things I do sometimes as I go to sleep is pray, "Lord, I'm going to be very relaxed over the next several hours, so You will be able to talk to me a whole lot better than any other time." Then I put my head on the pillow and go to sleep. I find it so much easier to hear from God when I'm asleep. The Holy Spirit has an opportunity to influence my subconscious. Many times, I wake up with the solution to a problem I've been working on consciously for weeks. Job 33:14–15 reads, "God speaks again and again, though people do not recognize it. He speaks in dreams, in visions of the night, when deep sleep falls on people as they lie in their beds" (NLT). I take that seriously and seek His voice even when reclined on the ground in a tent.

I dozed off but woke suddenly, hearing something outside my tent — and whatever it was, it wasn't small. Deep snuffling and the scuffle of paws on the ground indicated something big. My mind whirled. I had asked God to speak to me, but instead I was being visited by a large, wild creature!

What is it — a bear? A cougar? What do I do? Fire the gun? Do I have to be outside my tent first? What if it attacks me?

Unhelpfully, Annalee kept sleeping soundly in her tent. I heard her rhythmic breathing; she was probably dreaming of hot coffee and a pillow-top mattress. Meanwhile, the thing outside kept getting closer to my tent. I could not see through the walls, and anyway, it was 3 a.m. and there wasn't enough moonlight to discern even a shadow. Nearer it drew, the sounds of breathing and shuffling coming very close. Then I saw a snout — or something — push into my tent wall. I sat there terrified as it pulled its face back, then pressed it in a second time. The third time, not knowing what to do, I thought, *It can't see me. Maybe if I just punch it in the face as hard as I can, it will retreat.* Without giving it any more thought, I reared back and punched that creature in the face as hard as I could.

My fist slammed against a mushy bunch of cartilage, but I could not tell what kind of animal it was. Nevertheless, it ran off.

Maybe it was a javelina, I thought, picturing the big, wild pig common in that area. The creature's snout had been chest-high off the ground, but it didn't seem to act or sound like a mountain lion. *Maybe it was a bear,* I thought, reconsidering its size.

Apparently, I hadn't punched it hard enough, because within moments it was back. It shuffled over, checking my tent out again. I was upset. Hadn't I hit it squarely on the nose? Why wasn't it more afraid of me? Not knowing what else to do, I decided on the ridiculous, which at the time seemed rational: I took out my phone and started blaring my hiking music, beginning with Journey's "Separate Ways." This was followed by Survivor's greatest hits and other eighties classics which pumped me up on my uphill hikes during the day. Now they served an even better purpose — protection from wildlife.

Sure enough, the eighties hits drove that animal clear away! If you've ever doubted the power of good, classic rock and roll, doubt no more. It can literally control nature. Whatever that thing was, it left and didn't come back. But that was the end of my sleep that night.

The next day was comparatively uneventful, and we finally made it to our pick-up point and were taken to a nearby hotel for a normal night of sleep. Only there did I learn what had happened to the cowboy couple who had delivered water to us on the trail. As darkness fell, the trails were so narrow and the mountain sides so steep that they had gotten off the horses to lead them, so the animals wouldn't get spooked and take them both off a cliff.

Travis was a little ahead of Allison when he dropped his hat on the ground by accident. He leaned over to pick it up, but the horse didn't stop and nosed him off the cliff. This man fell thirty feet down the side of the mountain, badly hurt one of his ankles, and earned a solid case of road rash. He managed to stop at a precarious point, but was concerned about falling further. His hat was next to him, so he grabbed it and flipped it up as hard as he could, hoping to land it on the trail so Allison would find him. Before she did, he clawed his way back up the precipice, left the horse where it was, and limped out with a broken ankle. To make it worse, this cowboy was the same guy who bought us our trailer camper. Apparently, no good deed goes unpunished!

I wish his had been the last serious accident of our adventure, but in fact, the worst was yet to come.

CHAPTER 6

CRASHING THROUGH QUITTING POINTS

One of the coolest stories to take place at the SCDC in recent memory was when a group of make-believe superheroes became actual superheroes and rescued a girl from sex slavery.

One November, the Dream Center had big turkey giveaway. Awaken Church from San Diego came up and helped conduct a drive-through carnival where kids shot Nerf guns at targets and did other fun stuff. (Awaken Church is led by Jurgen and Leanne Matthesius, an outstanding Australian couple who moved to the U.S. in 2004 to start the church. Awaken now counts more than ten thousand people in weekly attendance. Our daughter, Aubrey, married the Matthesius' son, Ashly. Together, Ashly and Aubrey pastor our Phoenix campus.) One of the events was a superhero photo booth with guys dressed up like Captain America, Thor, and Green Arrow. Thor — a muscular, six-foot-four pastor from Awaken — was especially impressive, wearing his cape and holding a hammer. Kids stood with them and took photos.

After the event that night, there was a knock at the door of the Dream Center. It was a teenage girl.

"I sneaked out of the house," she told our people. "I don't want to be his sex slave anymore."

She was referring to the seventy-two-year-old man who bankrolled her family's house and was her husband by arranged marriage. He paid for everything — cars, toys, electronics — in exchange for having a wife nearly sixty years younger than he was. Now she wanted someone to go back to the house with her so she could get her important things, and leave.

Our people didn't know exactly what to do. They called the marshal's office but were told, "We can't get involved because no crime is reported." However, the marshal was willing to show up and stand by in case anything got ugly. So our guys put a little squad together, including the short-term missionaries from Awaken Church who had played Thor and Captain America earlier. It didn't hurt that a couple of them were Special Forces military veterans as well. Several women were on the team, and together they accompanied this teenage girl to her house, which was actually her prison. On the way there, she told our workers, "I'm going to be so embarrassed if he's in the back room watching his movies." She meant his pornography.

Arriving at the house, the marshal told our guys, "You have twenty minutes. We're there to help you escort her in, get her stuff, and get out. We're not there for a long conversation."

Our guys walked in with the girl and stationed themselves in the kitchen and hallway while she went back to her room with a couple of trash bags to retrieve her stuff. Her aged husband called out to ask what she was doing.

"I'm grabbing my stuff and leaving," she replied.

With that, "Thor" moved a little way down the hallway to be a presence. He watched this girl put her possessions in the bag, many of them toys and electronics. As with many girls who have been sexually abused, her mental development had stalled at a lower level of maturity.

Without incident, she left the house, and our team took her to the home of an aunt and uncle. They were supportive and stable, and very happy she had chosen to flee. It was a special moment of hugs and the beginning of a different kind of life for her.

Our guys had been fake superheroes by day and real ones by night. That girl's "husband" went to jail, and the girl's parents were charged with crimes for what they had put her through.

It is, as one team member called it, a "terrible privilege" to rescue people in those kinds of situations.

HARD MINISTRY

Our team had seen many crazy situations and damaged girls restored by that time, throughout all our facilities. Sex-trafficked girls come into recovery programs with a lot of hang-ups. There are almost always drug addictions, plus medical and psychological problems most people can't even imagine. As a result, these girls are not well-behaved. They will punch, slap, and throw up on you when you try to help them. The glamor of rescuing victims of human sex trafficking disappears really quickly, and you won't stick with it if you're not called to do it.

But this work touches my heart deeply. Every life matters to Jesus. Every girl is someone's daughter. Every girl can become a sister in Christ. That's what motivated me: hearing the stories of rescued girls who allowed God's redemption, forgiveness, and grace to transform them. I thought of the annual service our church holds, known as the "parade of ministries," when members of all our ministries walk across the front of the auditorium as people cheer them on. It's so energizing to see people from a couple of hundred ministries walk by. When formerly sex-trafficked girls walk across the stage wearing shirts that say "Survivor" and singing songs like "Waymaker," there isn't a dry eye in the place, including my own.

After the Mazatzals, Annalee and I were scheduled to pass by Lake Roosevelt, where 150 people from our church were going to meet us. The lake is less than two hours from Phoenix, and that would be the first time we had seen that many people since we had left for our trip. It also meant we had made it past the halfway point. That itself was a huge relief.

On a normal day, Annalee and I saw nobody on the trail. Hikers knew there was virtually no water that year. Ninety-nine percent of the time, we had the trail completely to ourselves. The only exception I remember was a "thru-biker" named Sean on a bicycle. We kept seeing him, and he told us he was doing the entire AZT on two wheels. At odd times he showed up, we greeted one another, and then he was gone again.

"Maybe he's a trail angel," we joked one day, imagining that he was looking after us. Only later did we seriously consider that it might be true.

We began our descent to the lake area where our people were gathered; the body of water looked so grand and refreshing. A long, arched bridge spanned it, and our friends met us in cars and on foot to cheer and walk across the bridge with us. What an amazing feeling to suddenly be slapping high-fives and hugging people we hadn't seen for weeks! After an empty trail, it was like walking into a whirlwind of pure encouragement.

Someone handed me a bullhorn, and I gave a quick report of our trip thus far. Annalee thanked them for their support, and we encouraged them to keep supporting the greater cause, the Short Creek Dream Center, and telling others about what we were accomplishing there. Our story was getting traction by now, and many of the people were wearing "Adventure Your Life" T-shirts, which was the theme of our effort. We took many selfies with people and kids that day and felt honored by their presence. We signed autographs for young people, which seemed a little strange, but they had great admiration for what we were doing. It was epic to them. For me, it brought back to mind the seriousness of what we were doing — raising a lot of money for such a worthy cause.

We still had ten miles to go that day, and the sun was setting earlier each evening, so after half an hour or so they bid us farewell. Silence returned as the lonely trail became our only companion once again. To make it harder, the first stretch was straight up a mountainside which formed one edge of the bowl of the lake area. With no creeks running and no other lakes along the path, we ran out of water and had to avail ourselves of the briny-looking liquid in a massive round cattle trough we found.

I cannot believe I'm drinking this stuff, I thought, putting all my faith in the filter.

Bristling cat claw — a thorny bush — overhung the trail and grabbed our arms and legs, causing us to bleed. The barbs did more than scrape; they went in deep, like hooks, then pulled out. As Annalee recorded later, "Trail was very difficult to follow — got lost and had to bushwack a bunch."

This was one of the places I had to crash through some quitting points. Runners know what quitting points are. It happens on mile twenty-four of a marathon. Your side is aching, your feet throbbing, and everything in you says, "Quit." But you don't. You keep running.

Employees know what quitting points are. Your boss brings in another assignment and lays it on top of a huge stack of uncompleted assignments. Or he promotes your "enemy" to be your boss. You want to say, "I quit," but you don't.

Husbands and wives know what quitting points are. We all have been tempted to quit on each other sometimes, but we soldier through to better times.

Quitting points pop up all the time. In our family, quitters are not allowed. One of my dad's sayings growing up was, "There is nothing worse than a quitter." We never gave ourselves an "out." Once you started an adventure, project, or endeavor, you were going all the way. That was drilled into us. We could be "wanna-quitters," but only if we knew we wouldn't actually quit.

James 1:12 (GW) says, "Blessed are those who endure when they are tested. When they pass the test, they will receive the crown of life that God has promised to those who love him." (GW) Rather than complaining about quitting points, we were taught to be thankful for the opportunity to overcome them!

There's a challenge. Maybe that's why I get so fired up whenever I see someone who refuses to quit — because deep inside, I want that to be true of me. My heart is drawn to people who have a fire in their spirit that won't be quenched.

There was an amazing display of endurance at the 1984 Summer Olympics, when Gabriella Anderson, after running 25.75 miles, staggered into the Los Angeles Coliseum exhausted, dehydrated, and disoriented. It took her nearly six minutes to finish the final few hundred meters of that marathon. While commentators in their plush, air-conditioned booths questioned the wisdom of someone who had pushed her body to the brink, Gabriella inspired hundreds of millions of viewers as she gave the whole world an object lesson on perseverance.

She crashed through a massive quitting point.

When you and I crash through our quitting points, we don't always feel a lot of slaps on our backs. You won't necessarily hear angels singing. But you and God will know you did it, and He says you will be blessed for it.

When I was nine years old, I played Little League baseball. One day I stormed off the field during practice because I was mad at my coach. After I had walked five miles home, my dad learned that I had disrespected the coach and my team — and, worst of all, that I had quit. I assure you, he taught me a painful lesson that day. I really thought he had gone overboard with his response, so I asked him, "Dad, why did you freak out on me for that?" He said, "Son, you don't understand. If I let you quit on baseball just because things got a little tough, then one day when things get tough in school, you'll quit. And when seasons get difficult in your marriage you'll quit on that. And when a crisis comes in your life, you'll want to quit on God. I know you feel like quitting, but you are going to stick with this because there is a lot more at stake than just baseball."

My dad was always teaching us to crash through quitting points like that. When I was a kid, I'd go jogging with him because I loved being with him no matter what he was doing. We would set our goal and say, "We're going to run four miles. That's sixteen laps around the track." Off we would go, my little legs barely keeping up with his. On about lap sixteen, I would want to quit because I was worn out, but I would always keep going. Just as we crossed the finish line, he would sometimes say, "Don't stop Luke — let's go one more. I know you can do it." I hated that, but he was trying to teach me a lesson: Quitting points are not brick walls. They are tissue paper. They are meant to be crashed through.

CRASHING THROUGH ADDICTION

My mom crashed through a major quitting point in recent years. She went through a season in which she suffered from panic attacks. Doctors medicated her with drugs, and she became dependent on them. Not only that, but the pain of her past ambushed her during that season as well. Mom was born in Finland during World War II. The only recollection she has of her biological parents was when she was two or three years old, watching her father chase her mother through the house with an ax, trying to kill her. He failed at that, then went off and died in the war. My mother's mother couldn't care for her properly, so for a time, my mom lived on the streets of Helsinki, developing rickets — a softening of the bones in children due to malnutrition — and suffering in many ways.

Lots of Swedes adopted orphans from Finland at that time, and my mom was adopted by the fire chief of Stockholm. She lived a wonderful life in Stockholm, but remained a very nervous, panic-prone person. She was also a beauty queen and competed in the Miss Sweden pageant. She was gorgeous.

Mom came to America as an flight attendant, and in San Francisco, a friend took her to my dad's revival meeting. She got saved that night. She remembers that when she got to the altar, Dad ran there fast to pray with her. They were married just a few months later, but it's a miracle their marriage survived. They had almost nothing in common, culturally. Mom had come from a lifestyle of parties and worldly living, and now found herself in a Pentecostal denomination which didn't even allow her to wear makeup. At one point, she packed her bags and went back to Sweden, but then returned and she and my dad made it work.

When my brother, Matthew, was eighteen and went to Los Angeles to help found the Dream Center, Mom became so concerned for him that all those emotions from her past returned. She began having panic attacks. Doctors prescribed strong medication, which led to her addiction. She became absolutely stuck in chemical dependency, and I confess I thought she would never get out of it. But God had a plan to set her free, and today my mom is completely free of addiction and has greater peace than ever before.

She crashed through such a major quitting point. My mom is amazing.

Think about it: We don't admire people who overcome small challenges or take the easy way out. We admire those who face big giants and emerge victorious.

In fact, I have discovered that whenever God gets ready to channel His dream through somebody, He doesn't always choose the boldest, most intelligent, or prettiest person. More often than not, God looks for someone who simply won't quit. He looks for those who will take the journey from the impossible to the incredible. Our God delights in defying human logic. Every person in the Bible who accomplished something extraordinary faced the word "impossible." Abraham's calling was impossible. Moses's calling was impossible. Esther's assignment was impossible. David beating Goliath was impossible. As Daniel faced the lion's den, as Shadrach, Meshach, and Abednego faced the fiery furnace, as Job faced devastation, as Stephen faced the stones, as Peter faced his failure, as Jesus faced the cross, as the Church faced Rome — it was all impossible. From cover to cover, the Bible is full of God's dreams, which always began with the word "impossible."

That's why we often face impossibilities — because God thinks highly of us! He is calling us to His normal standard, which is the journey from the impossible to the incredible. When we hit an impossible situation regarding our health, career, marriage, kids, or anything else, we are being invited onto this journey of overcoming.

As for me and Annalee in the middle of a path criss-crossed by thorny branches, "impossible" seemed just about the right word — or at least "highly unpleasant." By the time we finally met our team at the next pick-up point, we were fuming over what we had been through. As if on cue, we arrived at the hotel and saw firefighters sleeping there after combatting nearby wildfires. That put things back into perspective and we got our attitudes in check again.

We were heading into another three-day stretch in the wilderness, so that night at the hotel, we packed nine meals for the coming days, plus water.

"This is a lot of weight," I told Annalee.

She made a face that said, *Yes, but we don't have another option.*

Leaving water behind wasn't possible just because streams weren't flowing. So we laid everything out and took a good hour to make sure it was all ready. Then we packed, cinched and jammed the contents of our backpacks down tight, crawled into bed, and slept, hoping to heal up.

A few days earlier, a man in a prayer meeting at our church in Phoenix had had a vision. In it, a boulder rolled forward and an angel put a hand out to stop it. The man shared what he'd seen with others, but I didn't learn about it till later. What he had seen was about to become a reality.

CHAPTER 7

LIFE IN THE BALANCE

Annalee was excited about the next section of the trail, the Superstition Mountains, because at end of the first day we would pass through an abandoned orchard on one of the peaks. But we had lots of elevation to gain to get there, and this day presented fresh challenges while I was still recovering from the old ones. It also included the five-hundred-mile mark of our trip. We had hiked thirty straight days, something I didn't know I was capable of. We were carrying two days' worth of water through a punishing five thousand feet of elevation gain. Most of the time I was able to buck myself up, but this day felt especially torturous.

We rose early, and our team took us to the closest place to the trail they could reach. Sleep had been good, but not good enough. I was worn out from the day before, our limbs still cut up and tender from the briars.

"There you go," our team members said. "Have a great day. See you in a few."

Annalee and I stepped onto the trail with our bulging backpacks, and saw directly ahead of us a path which seemed to head straight uphill.

Oh, my gosh, I can't do this, was my first thought. But we trudged on.

It was a rural road, and deer hunting had just begun. Guys in hunting buggies drove by and waved at us. How badly I wanted to hop aboard and gain a few easy miles! But the air was cool enough — eighty degrees or so — and the day was overcast. We took every kindness we could get.

We pushed through those steep miles and came down the backside of the mountain, only to see another massive climb ahead of us. Between us and it was a no-man's land we later learned has a name: "The Big Dip." As we descended into it, I looked up to see another actual hiker emerge out of nowhere and pass us going the opposite direction. We waved at each other but didn't stop to talk. It was so rare to see other people that the incident stuck in my mind.

We had gone beyond the hunters on their buggies and were approaching a big wash. By now, the trail had disappeared into a hard pan of rock. It felt like walking on dust-covered concrete.

"Whoa," we both said more than once as we slipped and almost fell. The unwieldy backpacks made it tough to retain a stable center of gravity, and I had to grab things to keep upright when the trail steepened.

"Be very careful," I told Annalee for the first time on the trip. "Focus. Watch your step."

I didn't want one of us to twist an ankle and get into a rescue situation way out there in that seemingly endless expanse.

THE ACCIDENT

To reach the bottom of the wash, we repeatedly lowered ourselves with our hands through the rocks. Our minds were fully engaged, constantly choosing the right landing spot for our feet. Annalee was in front of me, earphones in and listening to music. I more or less emulated her movements — or improved on them as I could — from behind her.

She stepped past a large boulder, and I followed a few steps behind, putting my hand on the stone for balance as I lowered myself down. It was about a four-foot drop. When my feet hit the ground, I was below the boulder with my hand still on it.

That's when I felt it move.

Life slowed down. I saw Annalee directly below the wavering boulder, oblivious of the danger. Instinctively, I yelled, "Annalee, get out of the way!" I half-lunged, pushing her aside while my other hand remained on the boulder, which was now directly behind me. It had come unstuck from the steep ground and was moving toward me. There was no avoiding it. I felt the mass of seven thousand pounds of rock hit me full on as I faced it. It slid over me and I fell to the ground, at its mercy.

I toppled forward, shoved face-down into the mountainside. The behemoth seemed to draw me into its cavernous mouth as it proceeded downhill. The rock — seven feet wide and four feet thick — had a concave area at its front, and this enveloped me. Its solid mass drove my flesh against the hardpan rock. Annalee now stood safely to the side, though the gigantic slab had managed to scrape her knee on the way past.

"Dear Jesus, help me," I prayed as the rock ground me before itself. It was not rolling but sliding, and threatening to pull my head underneath it. The uneven, rocky ground acted like a giant mill, pulverizing me. I felt countless rocks and jagged places in the terrain as the boulder chewed at me, snapping my forearm, breaking my ribs, and mangling my leg.

This is life or death, I thought. *If it rolls over me or catches my head, I'm done. It's lights-out.*

The dance of death seemed to go on forever. I felt more bones breaking, felt my hand go under the rock, felt the boulder riding my legs and back. My left leg got tucked under my body, and the weight of the boulder bent it to the breaking point. I knew I was being badly injured, and the pain was beyond what I thought possible. I waited for the unthinking beast to finally strike my head and finish me off.

"Dear God, help me!" I cried out again and again.

Eight seconds passed after the boulder broke loose, and then it somehow stopped on the steep grade and teetered like a seesaw, pivoting off my broken body. The boulder had been halted by a small rock about the size of a volleyball. There's no way that should have happened, but it did. Annalee stood, immobilized and watching. The thing had not finished me off after all. It was being held in place above me.

"'Get me out of here!" I hollered, or thought I did. To Annalee, it sounded like incomprehensible screaming. I heard the scuffling of her feet coming toward me. She whispered a prayer under her breath, then saw me alive beneath the concave portion of the rock. Immediately, she grabbed my backpack straps and pulled me downhill and to the side, with the help of gravity. We both knew the slab was so precarious that it could roll again at any moment.

I lay there, broken, on the ground. My backpack was in shreds. It had taken much of the impact. I was out of immediate danger — but what had happened to my body? Annalee asked me questions to determine how badly injured I was.

"Can you breathe? Can you move your fingers and toes? What hurts?" she asked.

Everything, I wanted to say, but topping the list were my groin, my leg, my right hand, and my forearm. My chest and back hurt badly, too, but my hip did not hurt, even though I couldn't lift my left leg. Annalee examined my right hand. A nasty, bone-deep gash had partially severed my middle finger, and the skin was stripped from the back of my hand. Blood was coursing from it. My left forearm was already swollen like a baseball.

I glanced back at the boulder. *Why did it stop?* I wondered. It was like something had halted its inevitable slide and held it there to the mountain. One complete roll, and Annalee would have been dealing with my corpse.

"Dad, hold your hand up," she said. I could see that the amount of blood flowing from the gash would soon drain me of life. I held it up and the bleeding soon stopped. But my position on the ground was so awkward that I could barely breathe.

"Annalee, wedge your sleeping pad under my back," I gasped.

She tried to do as I asked, but moving my body even an inch inflamed every painful part. She also had to move some of the big rocks I was lying on.

"It's fine," I cried out. "Just don't touch me."

We both had the same unspoken thought: *Was I bleeding internally?*

Annalee pulled out the Garmin InReach, hit the SOS button, and composed a short text to Atwood, our risk manager at the church. It read: "BLDR ON DAD." I thought how we had given Atwood such a hard time for making us take a satellite phone on the trail.

"We don't need a sat phone," I had scoffed at him good-naturedly. "We don't need helicopter insurance. You worry too much."

But he had insisted: "You are going to take a satellite phone and we're going to get the helicopter insurance."

"That's a waste of money," I insisted, but he was unyielding. So we'd packed that extra weight in the form of a satellite phone we were sure we would never use. Now, Annalee was squatting next to me, sending SOS messages to the outside world as if my life depended on it — which it probably did.

"I'm too far down the mountain. I can't get a signal to call him," she said.

We both knew she would have to ascend to higher ground to place a call that might save my life.

"Go," I said with as much peace and confidence as I could summon.

She had already shed tears, but now she began to openly cry.

"I'll be back, Dad," she told me. The thought passed through both of our minds: *Would I be alive when she returned?*

We couldn't know. Off she went up the side of the mountain.

Is he going to bleed out while I'm gone? she kept asking herself. Tears fell with every footstep. She tried to keep her mind from imagining what she would find when she returned.

Finally, she reached the saddle, weeping with exertion. She knelt for a quick moment in the dirt.

"God, be with us, protect us, help us," she prayed. Calm blanketed her for the first time since the accident, and with a broad, blue sky above us she called Atwood, hoping he would pick up.

Meanwhile, down at the scene of the accident, I lay busted up beyond imagination. It had been nice and cloudy all day, providing cover from the piercing sun. Now the clouds cleared away and the sun beat down on my bleeding, bruised body. I couldn't even move to a shady spot.

Then I had what I consider to be a very Barnett kind of thought.

Am I just being wimpy right now? I wondered. *I've seen guys in wars go through worse than this. If I had to hike out of here, could I do it? If I can somehow stand up maybe I can finish the day. I'm going to try.*

Mustering my resolve and strength, I tried to lift myself up. Pain shot through me so convincingly that I lay back down again. But I wasn't done.

Don't give up so soon, I told myself. *Maybe I can just get to my feet.*

I tried again but pain wasn't the only obstacle. My body simply wouldn't respond to my directions. I could hardly move.

Then something strange happened, which really got my attention: all the color went out of my vision. The world around me turned black and white.

Am I dying? I wondered. *Am I having a stroke? I don't want to die here. There's so much I want to accomplish in life. There are kids and grandkids I want to see. God, help me.*

Great peace flooded my heart as I considered that this might be my moment to go, but still I closed my eyes and prayed, "God, I don't want to die here. There's so much to be done."

Either I fell asleep or I lost consciousness due to shock, but twenty minutes later I heard Annalee return. I opened my eyes and color had returned.

"Dad! Dad!" she yelled, coming carefully down the steep hardscape. "I reached someone. They're trying to send a helicopter. I'll need to send them coordinates."

A helicopter — wow, I thought. We had rolled our eyes when Atwood insisted on rescue insurance. Now the prospect of being airlifted out provided the greatest sense of relief. Atwood suddenly seemed to me like the smartest guy on the planet.

Annalee sat beside me and looked me over to ascertain my current condition.

"Do you need more water?" she asked, and put a hat on my head to shade my face from the sun. Then she fished Advil from her pack and put a couple in my mouth. I was able to swallow them. She spotted a couple of easy-to-move rocks under my body and pulled them out from under me. Then she grabbed a bottle for herself and went back up the mountain to make sure her messages to Atwood were going through.

When she returned, we waited, listening for the rotor blades of the helicopter which, we hoped, would arrive soon to take me to safety.

"Dad, I just want to pray for you," she said and laid hands on me. "God, heal his body. Get us through this. Amen."

There was silence for a while, and then I suggested something.

"Annalee, you should record what just happened on your phone," I said.

"Dad, why are you even thinking of this right now?" she replied.

"We have to tell this story," I said. "We're in it right now. Let's use the time and at least make a record of what's happening."

So she moved right next to me and began to take video, explaining what had happened, that I was alive and not paralyzed, and that we didn't know the extent of my injuries. The video didn't last long, but it captured a few moments of a very real situation.

When she was done, she added, "I'm sorry this happened, Dad."

"Oh, Annalee, I'm sorry to ruin your hike," I said.

"That doesn't matter," she said. "You didn't ruin my hike. I feel like I ruined you."

It occurred to me, even in the state I was in, that looking ahead with vision would pull us toward the future better than dwelling on what had just happened.

"Annalee, you are not to blame for this," I said, still very weak. "I wanted to do this hike with you. The Bible says rains falls on the just and the unjust. But here's what I think: I think you have to finish this hike. I think we have to find someone to finish this with you."

She wiped her fresh tears away and looked at me like I might be in shock.

"I don't want to finish the hike," she said. "If you're done, I'm done."

I pressed her, "Annalee, people across America have sponsored us to finish this hike. It has to go on. It looks like I can't finish it, but you have to go on. People are counting on us."

"I don't want to," she protested. "I don't feel like it.

I let my silence persuade her. After a while she said with real resolve, "Dad, I'll do it."

That was the Annalee I knew. Somehow it seemed right to think this way, not to let the setback define our trip. She was smiling at me now. I hoped it was a reflection of my condition and her sense of hope in the face of what had happened.

"You seem more alert than before," she told me.

I'm happy just to be alive, I wanted to say.

Then we heard blades whirring overhead.

RESCUED

Annalee leapt to her feet and got out her headlamp to use as a signaling device, waving it at the aircraft. It circled nearby, and it took a while for Annalee to attract the crew's attention. She finally got a text to them saying, "We're right under you." They spotted us, but there was nowhere to land. Beneath the chopper's body, a line appeared, and a medic attached to it came down to the ground, carrying a stiff board.

"I'm Ed. How are you?" he said, introducing himself to Annalee. "Where's your dad?"

They hiked to where I was, and he greeted me with, "Hey, I'm Ed," as if we had met for coffee in suburban Phoenix.

"I'm going to check you out," he continued. "Is your mouth tingling? Do you know who you are? What's the date? Can you move your fingers?"

He set the board down by me as he kept asking me questions. He gently took my wrist and felt my pulse.

"I have to get you on this board," he said. "Then I'll wrap a bag around you and attach you to the line with me. The pilot will lift us three hundred yards over to a flat spot and we'll put you in the helicopter. We'll take you to a wilderness trauma center, and they'll put you in another helicopter and take you out of here. But first, we have to roll you on your side and slide this board underneath you. It's going to hurt, so bear with us."

With Annalee's help, Ed moved my body inch by inch onto the board, over the uneven ground. The mountainside was steep and Annalee kept sliding downward. The pain of my body moving was nearly enough to make me pass out. When Annalee looked at me, her face blanched as if mirroring mine.

Their efforts got me onto the board, but it was on rocks which were very slick. The medic stood downslope with the board — and me on it — resting against his shins to keep it from taking off like a sled.

"Annalee, put your hands under your dad's chin and hold him while I wrap this bag around him," Ed said. This was the plan for keeping me from sliding downhill while both my body and the backboard were put into a bag-like covering.

Annalee dug her heels in and held me steady by my chin while Ed maneuvered the bag around my body. The operation took ten minutes because he was trying not to hurt me, for which I was grateful.

"Annalee, I don't know what we would do if you weren't here," Ed said when he'd finished. He strapped the bag shut around me, tied a rope to it, and radioed the chopper to come over. The only visibility I had now was through a hole in the bag less than a foot wide. The world disappeared except for the bright blue sky.

The small rescue helicopter hovered overhead and dropped the line. Ed clipped the cable to the bag, and himself to the cable above me. I began to feel flutters of fear for the flight that lay ahead, but that fear was overwhelmed by a simple desire to get medical help.

"We're going to take you over to a clearing on a nearby hill," Ed repeated to me through the opening in the bag. "Then we'll put you in the chopper itself and fly you to a remote trauma center. From there, they'll take you to a hospital. Annalee, we will send a helicopter back to get you because there isn't room in this one."

"Okay," she said bravely, but I could hear a slight tremble in her voice.

Then we lifted off. While in flight, Ed leaned over from above and spoke to me.

"We have to drop you when we get there, and the pilot will try to be gentle, but there will be a little jar when you hit the ground," he warned.

I dreaded that *thunk*, but there was nothing for it. The bag was warm, the sky was clear, and a paramedic was there to help me. Things were getting better.

Then I hit the ground, and every scintilla of pain in my body shouted at once. At that point I closed my eyes and tried to quit caring what happened to me. Ed moved quickly, unhooking, lifting me. He and the pilot picked the board up with me on it and put me in the helicopter. Ed opened the aperture a little bit so I could see my surroundings. It was indeed a very small aircraft. Up we went, zooming off to the trauma center.

Somewhere behind us was Annalee, alone, waiting for her own rescue.

Left Behind

Watching us go, Annalee felt a measure of relief at Ed's assurance that the helicopter would come back for her. She had been expecting to hike out on her own, so now all she had to do was wait. That was its own challenge for someone who had just seen a large boulder nearly roll over her father.

Wind from the helicopter rotors had scattered our stuff into bushes and rocks around the accident site, so Annalee busied herself gathering it all. Then she found a spot in the shade, pulled up a notes app on her phone, and began journaling about what was happening. She had journaled every day already. Putting her thoughts in writing and laying out the simple facts felt healthier than replaying the worst elements of what had just happened.

Emotions roiled inside her. She wanted to deny what had happened. Then she was angry that our trip was ending this way. She didn't really like my suggestion that she finish the hike without me; even less did she like just giving up and throwing in the towel. She typed out her thoughts as she waited.

Maybe they forgot me, she wondered after a while. Nearby bushes rustled — just the wind. Annalee looked at her bag, which held a small pistol. *There are wild animals out here*, she thought. *My dad punched one in the nose*. Wind enlivened the bushes again and she considered getting the little pistol out, then decided just to wait. She worried that a mountain lion or bear would smell the blood and come looking for an easy meal.

Soon enough, about an hour after it had left, the chopper whirred into view, hovered over the nearby valley, and sent down another line with Ed attached to it. Annalee grabbed my bag, torn and spilling, and whatever else she could carry and marched down the hill.

"Your turn," Ed said, grinning, when she got there. His lightness of heart dispelled much of the concern Annalee felt about me. Not only that, but the helicopter ride proved more exciting than expected. They had taken off the doors to fit me and the board, and after picking up Annalee, the crew zoomed to a neighboring hilltop to retrieve them. Then they set course for the wilderness trauma center where I was receiving the most blessed painkillers imaginable.

DOWN THE MOUNTAIN

The wilderness "trauma center" turned out to be a large paramedic van — but that was enough. The helicopter landed at a place called Canyon Lake and the crew brought me out on the stiff board. Nurses and medics rushed to me on every side, each with a task to fulfill. One checked my pulse, another my eyes, another my fingers, and another set my neck to make sure my spine wasn't affected. More pain flared as they transferred me to an actual gurney, and then they started an IV which took the sharp edge off any sensations.

"He's stable. Let's get him to Scottsdale," they said, referring to the hospital and trauma center which would become my home for the foreseeable future.

They wheeled me from the van to another helicopter, and in those moments, I imagined I heard a voice I recognized.

"Hang in there, Luke, you're going to make it," it said. My head was strapped to the bed, but with my eyes I glanced around and spotted the face of Atwood, our risk manager. He had been with us in the hotel the night before, helping us to pack. Now he was by my side.

How did he get up here so fast? I wondered.

Atwood has been a member of our church since I was just a kid. His encouraging words — and his very presence — caused gratitude and love to swell up in my heart. He had come all this way to reassure me. It also meant Annalee would be cared for in my absence.

He put his hand on my shoulder.

"Pastor, we love you and we're praying for you," he said. "You're going to be fine and you're going to make it."

Then I was whisked away. Atwood may never know how much that moment ministered to me. It was better than medicine to have someone who loved and knew me by my side. I say now what I felt like saying then: Atwood, I love you very much. That moment will mark me forever.

The sound of accelerating rotors filled my ears again — my third and final flight of the day, this time bound for Scottsdale Osborne Hospital Trauma, the highest-level trauma hospital in the state. There I would find out just how badly my body was broken — and what would happen next.

A Father's Story

Meanwhile, in Minneapolis, my dad was scheduled to speak at a special church service. A young couple leading a relatively new suburban church had bid on an old, historic church campus in the city and gotten it, despite the fact that several other potential buyers were interested in it, too. The building boasted a balcony, cherry wood, stained-glass windows, and paintings that seemed to be masterpieces. To dedicate the facility, the couple asked my dad to preach three times on the congregation's first Sunday meeting there. Dad has always maintained that the best place for a church is downtown because a city's downtown embodies its culture. History shows that when the downtown area deteriorates, the city does, too — and then, the state. But when a downtown area experiences revival or revitalization, life radiates out to the suburbs and the entire region.

The young couple met Dad at the airport and took him straight to the building, excitedly showing him all the cool features and telling him how God had led them to buy the campus. The group had just come from viewing the stained-glass windows and gorgeous paintings when Dad's assistant, Gary Blair, got a phone call from Joe Martinez, my right-hand man.

"Gary, a boulder rolled over Luke on the trail and a helicopter is on the way ... but he might not make it," Joe said.

Gary quickly relayed this information privately to my dad, who was stunned and could hardly believe what he was hearing. Then he had to make a choice. This young couple was so excited about him being there. They were treating him like royalty because this was a big weekend for their congregation to dedicate the downtown church campus. Would Dad fly back to Phoenix on a Saturday night to be near me, or would he keep the ministry commitment and fly back after speaking the next day? Being a Barnett, I knew exactly what he would do.

Dad walked back to where they were waiting.

"Luke's been in an accident on the trail," he said as their faces registered surprise and alarm. "A boulder rolled on top of him and he's in a fight for his life. Let's pray right now."

Without another word, they all clasped hands and joined in fervent prayer for me. When they finished, Dad said, "Let me tell you what we're going to do: we are going to continue as planned. It's going to be a great weekend that will bring glory to the Lord for what He is doing here."

Trusting my dad, the couple agreed. That night they took him and some church leaders to an expensive dinner at a local steakhouse, a real sacrifice for them financially. Dad talked with everyone and acted like nothing had happened. Then they took him back to his hotel room, where he immediately tried to call Angel but couldn't reach her. Then he threw himself face-first across the bed and began to cry out in prayer.

"God, please spare him. I want to go home but this is Kingdom business and You'll take care of Luke," he said.

He knew people would question why he didn't catch the first flight home, but instead preach three services on Sunday before returning to Phoenix. But an old and true story that is part of our family's heritage explained his mentality — and when Dad arrived at the airport in Phoenix the next day, he did something he seldom does and jumped on Instagram to share it with his followers.

He said, "When I was born, my dad was an evangelist. He often had no place to stay but the parsonage. He and my mother had a baby — me — and they decided my mother and I would stay at my grandmother's house. I was less than a year old. My grandaddy was an oil pumper for Magnolia, working in the Wagner Ranch, the second-largest ranch in the world. The house was way out away from civilization. The porch had a swing, and we would sing songs there at night. We could see the lights of the nearest city about ten miles away."

He continued, "Dad was in Granite City, Illinois, preaching a great revival that the leaders kept extending week after week. But I came down with a severe type of pneumonia. The doctor didn't know if I could live or not. He informed us that this could take my life. I was a baby about to die. They contacted my dad. The revival was so great that one of the bartenders in town said if they didn't run this preacher out of town, the bars would go out of business. This big building was packed night after night, my dad preaching hellfire, people running to the altars. He called home and told my mom, 'I want to come home more than anything in the world, but I don't know if God would be pleased.' Then he hung up the phone and wept, saying, 'God, I want to see my son.' God spoke to him, 'If you put My work first, I'll take care of your work. If you take care of My things, I'll take care of your things.'"

Dad finished the story: "My father called back to relate what God had said. My mother didn't understand. Grandma got on the phone and gave him what-for, calling him coldhearted. Meanwhile, I as a baby got worse and worse. Finally, it didn't look like he would make it home in time to see me alive. He preached Saturday night, drove home all night, reached Electra, Texas, the closest town nearby, and as he was driving toward the house, the family doctor was coming the opposite way on the dirt road. As they passed each other, the doctor waved to my dad and shook his head as if to indicate that the situation was bad. 'Oh, I'm too late,' Dad said. He reached the house, slammed on the brakes, and ran in — and there I was crawling to him. The very night he closed that revival, I experienced a remarkable turnaround. That's why the doctor shook his head. He couldn't believe what had taken place."

That event and others like it define how our family lives. If we take care of God's work, we know He will take care of ours. It's a Barnett slogan we live by. How many times I have heard my dad preach on Proverbs 3:6, which says, "In all thy ways acknowledge him, and he will direct your paths" (KJV). There are twelve words in that passage. Six are our part, six are God's. My dad has spent his life going around bragging on God, and God has been faithful to take care of us in every situation.

Because all the hospitals were still locked down during that time due to fears over COVID, the trauma center would not let anyone but Angel in to see me. Like the rest of my family, Dad had to wait to hear reports from her or enjoy relatively brief conversations with me by phone.

Once he knew I would live, one of his main concerns was that I wouldn't be able to play golf again! He knew how much I enjoyed the game, and it broke his heart to think of my being incapable of doing one of the things I love most. He liked to brag on all his kids, and it was true that I competed well at tournaments. I won the Convoy of Hope tournament four times running and held a club record.

But all of that, along with a lot of other things, seemed to be gone in smoke while my future hung in the balance.

CHAPTER 8

A WIFE'S VIEW

As Luke's wife, you can bet I have my own perspective on what happened, so I'm adding a chapter to give you my side of the story.

First off, I was very concerned about Luke going on the trail with Annalee, probably more than I was concerned about Annalee herself. Luke is super-athletic — and I'm just going to say it: sexy — but this trail-hiking was a different kind of exertion. He's good on basketball courts and golfing greens, in workout rooms and air-conditioned gyms. Luke likes cities; he's called to minister in one, so that's a good thing. But sleeping, eating, and walking in the dirt are not on his list of favorite things.

Still, I admired him for committing to spend six weeks in unsanitized, unpredictable nature (did he mention the possibility of wild burros?) to protect our daughter and to raise money for the dearest place to my heart: Short Creek Dream Center in Colorado City. But a feeling of dread settled over me about the whole thing before it began. I prayed about it and handed it over to God, and that was the best I could do. Once a Barnett has latched onto a goal, it's hard to shake him or her off of it. These people make pit bulls look like sissies.

When the Grand Canyon kidney stone incident happened, I was

like, "Here we go. This is it." I got the call from Annalee while I was an hour's drive from the south rim.

"Dad's not doing well," she said. "He's about to pass out."

"Where are you now?" I asked.

"A few miles below the south rim," she said.

A few miles!? I thought. *That's a long way to walk and not pass out.*

"I'll have the team run water and an energy drink down," I told her, and pressed the pedal down. I called Grand Canyon security to ask them to deploy help. For whatever reason, they weren't that concerned or up to the task, so I arrived, parked the car, met our team, and recruited my son-in-law to run four miles down the trail with a bottle of reboosting amino acid influx for Luke. I would follow behind at a slower pace to meet them. Kaden took the elixir and bounded down the path. I started after him with a video crew in tow.

Would you believe that a park ranger stood in front of us, blocking our way?

"Ma'am, I can't let you go down there," he said. "The sun's going down. Do you have a flashlight?"

"No," I said. "Do you have a donkey?"

He seemed easily confused.

"No," he answered.

"Excuse me?" I said, raising my voice. "We have someone in a medical situation down there and you're offering me no help? Pardon me, please."

We walked past him, and he allowed himself to be ignored. He was right about one thing: the sun was indeed going down and there was no time to waste.

As we hurried down, we rounded a corner and encountered a herd of rams. I figured they were as tame as farm animals, and not wanting to break our pace, I charged right through them. I didn't find out until later that they were dangerous. Oh, well. They let us go right by.

Finally, we came to Luke and Annalee, three miles beneath the rim. I have to admit, Luke's appearance really shocked me. His face was gray and gaunt, his skin pasty enough to belong to a corpse. It seemed he was ready to pass out at any moment and I could tell his levels were way off. He needed water, sugars, amino acids, the whole boost.

Oh, Lord, I thought. *Are we going to have to call a helicopter right now?*

I tried to contain my emotions upon seeing him like that, and I guess a motherly reaction came out. I began doting on him. Of course, he didn't want that, so we all trudged up the trail together, Luke in great pain and me distressed by what was happening. Luke began by taking four-inch steps at a snail's pace. As we continued, he started to feel better, and amazingly his pace increased to almost normal speed.

Then the rescue crew became the rescued crew. Some of our video guys weren't in great shape and they had trouble going uphill. These guys typically spent their days in dark video-editing suites and were excited to be out in the action, but they hadn't exactly trained for this moment. All I heard was panting and gasping as they lugged their heavy equipment, and heavy selves, upward. One of them seemed to be hacking up a lung.

"Why did you guys even come down?" I asked, exasperated.

"It was good footage," one said.

"But now I'm rescuing you!" I replied.

I actually stayed back with them at their slower pace while Luke and Annalee used their burst of energy from the drink to press toward the rim. Bats were flying around us in the dark evening, and finally we all arrived safely at the top — even the video guys, who leaned over with their hands on their knees, sucking wind.

Luke and I knew he was passing a kidney stone, but we hadn't told Annalee yet so as not to alarm her. But now Luke was in so much pain and needed so much water that our team took him to an emergency clinic so he could replenish his fluid levels with an IV.

For my part, I breathed a big sigh of relief.

Alright, that was it, I thought. *That was our little trauma, our little dramatic situation. Now there won't be anymore. It'll all go smoothly.*

Those first few weeks of them on the trail had me wondering if Luke would finish. As a woman, and a planner, I couldn't help but think ahead to the possibility that he would drop out and Annalee would finish with a replacement partner. Behind closed doors, I even asked our team, "Okay, guys, what's Plan B if Luke comes off the trail?" I didn't doubt his stamina. I just knew this wasn't his thing — and seeing him ashen and suffering in the Grand Canyon confirmed that for me.

But when I hinted at a Plan B to Luke, he was adamant: "No, I committed to this. I'm finishing." So it was, and so I willed myself to believe that this kidney stone incident would be our only brush with danger.

THE CALL

The inspiring cause they were hiking for — restoring a broken community in Colorado City — was one to which I had given my life for the last several years. This ministry opportunity had come to us out of the blue. We knew it was a Heaven-sent assignment and I threw myself into it wholeheartedly. I organized what we did there, raised money as best I could, and told everyone about it. Not only that, but I was up there at the Short Creek Dream Center every couple of weeks, giving on-the-ground direction.

That's where I was when Annalee and Luke started into the wash that would define the trip, and our lives — at least for a while. A team of twenty young people had traveled six hours from our church to the Short Creek Dream Center to put on a creative arts workshop in the park. Their drama, dance, and music would brighten the community and allow local families to engage with the kids in a nonthreatening way. Parents would see their children being taught how to perform, and then their kids would entertain on the stage at the end. It was a great opportunity for them to interact with "outsiders" like us who were trying to serve their community.

Everything went awesomely well. We broke down barriers and built trust with families in the town that morning. Then it was time for the long journey home. It gets dark earlier in October, so my goal was to leave at noon and get home not long after dark. Usually, I travel alone, but this time a young lady named Hannah was with me. Hannah was in her mid-twenties, and we had known each other for years. She was mature and easy to talk to, and she made a good traveling buddy. I didn't realize how much I would need her in the hours to come.

Cell reception is poor in Colorado City, but early in the drive I started getting texts. The first one, from Atwood, read something like, "Luke has a cut on his arm that won't stop bleeding. They're air-evacuating him."

"That's an aggressive response for a bleeding hand," I said to Hannah. "Luke's not a guy to just take a helicopter out of the woods when he has a cut on his arm."

Right away, I was concerned. The facts didn't jibe with each other. If a helicopter was in the picture, then this was more serious than a cut. I knew my husband would walk out of a forest with a mangled limb before calling for help.

Reception disappeared as we drove the next stretch of lonely, two-lane highway until we got to Jacob Lake, a cute little log-cabin resort with a gas station. There I got my first voice call from Atwood.

"All I got from Annalee is she pushed the button to engage a helicopter, and something about a pretty bad bleed on his right hand from a rock," he said. "She's limited by the app she's using with the satellite phone."

I asked a few questions, but he had no more information.

"I'll get back to you as soon as we have more," he promised.

Hannah and I got back in the car, and our conversation turned a little intense. We tried to analyze what we had heard, projecting what might have happened. We were more than a bit concerned.

"Okay, his right hand and arm have been cut by a rock," I said. "So he can't safely stay overnight. Maybe there's risk of an infection? Maybe it's precautionary?"

A while later, another update arrived from Atwood. The accident was a little more serious than he had known and involved a pretty big rock. Atwood was heading to the helicopter at the wilderness trauma center and would be out of communication for a while. He turned me over to our oldest daughter, Aubrey, who would relay his intermittent messages to me while I was on the road.

Aubrey doesn't mind me saying she is the more dramatic of our children, and probably not my first choice to handle a crisis. I didn't want my emotions running any higher than they were, and I thought she would annoy the crud out of me with her lively responses to what was happening. Hannah's expression showed that she was thinking the same thing.

"Aubrey is going to lose it," I said, and Hannah nodded knowingly.

As it turned out, we were both wrong. Aubrey handled her sudden responsibilities like a champ. When she called us, she spoke calmly and evenly, and she prepped me before sharing bad information. Still, the tension in my body and mind increased with each mile and each new piece of information. Having Hannah in the car to look at texts as I drove the dangerous roads on the narrow highway toward Phoenix was a godsend.

I began to wonder, *How seriously is Luke's arm injured? Is the hand mangled? Are we talking permanent deformity? Lose a finger? Change our lives?*

When we got to Flagstaff and better reception, Aubrey called.

"Now, Mom, I've learned that this is quite a bit larger of a boulder and there might be broken bones involved," she said. "His leg was injured, too."

It started to make sense why a helicopter was needed. Luke's mobility was affected. He couldn't have walked out if he had wanted to — though I was willing to bet he had tried.

"His right hand might not be okay," she told me. "It may be crushed."

This was sounding worse with every communication. Back in the car, my conversation with Hannah turned to dire possibilities.

"Okay, we have a right hand forever injured," I stated. "That means no golf, no basketball. Things will change. The road he walks now is different. Barnett guys don't do anything but win. If anyone's going to have trouble getting over a deformity or handicap, it's Luke."

Then pictures came in. Hannah previewed them for me as I drove.

When an incoming message alert popped up, I handed my phone to her and said, "Do I want to see this?" She looked at them analytically and usually said, "Let's wait until we stop." She knew it wasn't smart to show the driver photos of her husband on the gurney with gashes, wires, and tubes all over him.

Then Annalee called and confirmed that Luke's leg was in jeopardy as well. I didn't want to pump her for information, unsure of her mental and emotional state. She tends to understate things anyway, so I knew I needed to wait to get a complete picture. Then I got a call from an unknown number and answered it. It was the ICU nurse with Luke in Scottsdale.

"Hello, is this Luke's wife?" he asked. I confirmed it was. "Luke was just wheeled in so I'm calling the first person on his ICE list," he went on. "He's got serious injuries. Breaks in leg, his arm, his hip, and a break in the neck of his femur."

A break in his neck? I thought. *Why didn't they tell me that sooner?*

"That sounds really bad. A broken neck," I said.

"The neck of his femur," the nurse corrected, but it didn't register with me. My head was swimming with facts and medical terms, and my mind stuck on "neck." When I got off the call, that major injury was all I could think about.

This is unbelievable, I thought, driving ever faster to get to Scottsdale and my battered husband. *If his neck is broken, this is a devastating emergency.*

NOT A ROCK — A BOULDER

By the time we arrived, every possibility seemed in play: loss of arm, loss of leg, compound fractures, internal bleeding and, in my understanding, a broken neck. It could hardly get worse without Luke dying or being paralyzed, and who knew when we might get that call?

I dropped Hannah off at her house with profuse thanks for her help and companionship that day. Then I beelined over to Scottsdale and Osborne Trauma Center to see for myself the true state of things.

Annalee and Atwood were there in the parking lot, along with other family members and some of the trail crew. This was during COVID lockdowns, and hospitals were not allowing anyone in. I rushed over to them and after hugs, they showed me a photo of the actual boulder that had done the crushing. That's when I realized how severe and life-threatening this all was. Calling it a "rock" did it no justice. This was a large slab of mountain that would kill anything it rolled over.

"Oh, my gosh," I said, and my level of concern soared.

Only one person was allowed to visit Luke that night, so I chose Annalee because I believed she needed to see her dad. She had been there when it happened. It was important for her to see that he was okay.

I knew Annalee could put up a tough exterior and pretend everything was fine even when it wasn't. She could hide stuff like an award-winning actress. While she was growing up, we had to watch her closely, and sometimes go after her pretty intensely to get her to share openly what she was really thinking. She knew how to internalize all her feelings. It wasn't deception, it was, "I've got this."

In the past, Luke would tell me, "Stop interrogating the child. She's fine." But pushing past the stoic facade was important at times so that Annalee would learn how to express herself and not get trapped inside with her feelings. In this case, I knew it was not humanly possible to be "fine" with whatever she had just experienced. She had seen her dad go under a sliding, multi-ton boulder, which had also narrowly missed her and in fact scraped her own knees. I knew she needed to get in there with him and see he was okay.

Apparently, the nurse heard our interaction when we walked in, because she quietly said, "Let's go against the rules and let you both come back." That was a small miracle in those days. We were ushered into the trauma unit on the bottom floor. There was Luke in a hospital gown, wired up, tubed up, and lying in a hospital bed. They had him on pain-killers, so he looked pretty good. His arm was wrapped in gauze, and his hand was still exposed as they had just finished stitching it up. He was dirt-free and looking alert for someone who'd gone through what he had just experienced. That put us very much at ease.

"Looks like they broke the rules and let you both in," he said with a smile.

"Don't tell anyone," I said. Annalee went over to him and gently touched his shoulder. We weren't allowed to have any more contact than that.

"How are you feeling?" she asked.

"Not too bad for having a big rock roll on me," Luke said, and they both smiled.

"I'm so glad you're okay," my little girl said.

"Me, too," he said. The love in their eyes for each other was every-thing a mother's heart could want. I knew that both needed to be built up to a place of strength again to get through what was still to come.

"Can you believe that big thing tried to come after us?" he said.

"It was coming after me until you shoved me out of the way," Annalee said.

"How's your knee?" he asked.

"It's fine," she said. "How's your hand?"

"Throbbing," he said. "Everything hurts, but it hurts less now."

To my surprise, they kept talking about the particulars of the incident, as if making sense of what had happened. I had been ready to avoid the subject, but they wanted to talk it through.

"How was it, being out there without me for a while?" Luke asked.

Annalee shrugged.

"Lonely," she said. "I had to pick up all our stuff from the bushes. The helicopter spread it around. It was a pain."

"Wasn't that helicopter ride cool, though?" he said.

"Yeah, I was happy when they showed back up," she replied.

They kept chatting, then looked ahead.

"Remember, Annalee, you've got to get out there and finish," Luke said.

For the first time, she didn't seem to like his suggestion. "I don't want to go on without you," she said. "I feel done."

"Barnetts aren't quitters," he said. "You have to finish this."

Having married into the Barnett family, I had often witnessed the near-biblical commitment they had to never quitting. Sometimes it seemed they would do anything to avoid this greatest of sins, but I realized it was a quality of high-capacity leaders. They simply took bigger risks than most people, raising the bar and doing things others considered dangerous. I believe it's part of what they are called to do, which helps to push the rest of us further. Barnetts are first-string guys — warriors. Now my daughter was being initiated into that commitment at a whole new level for her.

"If you were in this bed, you would want me to keep going," Luke continued. "Since I'm the one in this bed, it's up to you to finish it. We said we're going to do it, so we're going to do it."

I saw Annalee come around. She nodded her head and said, "I'll do it."

After that, Luke sighed and laid his head back. I knew he wanted the freedom to drift off. Plus, his surgery was scheduled for 7 a.m. the next morning. It was time for us to go. We couldn't hug him, so we each put a hand tenderly on his shoulder and said goodbye.

"I love you both. Thanks for coming to see me," he said.

"See you tomorrow," we said, and walked out of the hospital.

SUDDENLY HOME

Annalee seemed more settled after having seen her dad, but arriving at home threw her off kilter again. She looked at the house as if it were a foreign place.

"Everything okay?" I asked.

"Just weird to be home," she answered. "I was expecting to sleep in a tent in the Superstition Mountains tonight."

She sighed and set down her things. She told me later that it was difficult to fall asleep because the scene replayed in her mind and the blades of her ceiling fan reminded her of the helicopter rotors.

CHAPTER 9

SURGERIES START

It's Luke again, telling my own story — and let me say how much I appreciate Angel. She is simply the best, and I wouldn't choose anyone else to be my life partner. She is a warrior in her own right, and I'm glad she shared her perspective because an event like this involves many people.

When I arrived at the hospital, they put me in an MRI scan tube to discover everything that was broken. I had done my own self-diagnosis to keep myself occupied; I thought I had ripped my groin because it hurt so bad, broken a rib or two because breathing was so painful, knew I had broken my right arm because that was visible, and possibly done something to my left leg, which I couldn't move.

I came out of the tube and the doctor came in to give me the report.

"You have a broken forearm, three broken ribs, and you crushed your femur and broke a piece of your hip," he said.

Wow, I'm in worse shape than I thought, I thought.

"What about my groin muscle?" I asked him. "I must have torn it pretty badly because it's in such pain."

"No major damage to the groin," the doctor said. "The damage is in your hip and femur. The force of the accident pushed your femur through the hip bone, leaving a clean hole about the size of a quarter."

Man, I cannot believe this, I thought. *No wonder I couldn't move.*

"You've obviously got a big break in your forearm," he continued. "It snapped in half and the bones aren't even attached anymore. We'll see about putting a titanium rod through it. And we'll get your hand sewn up."

He didn't prolong the report, but scheduled surgery for the next day. Then someone came in to stitch up my finger and hand. That didn't take long, and I was wheeled into a shared recovery room to wait for a room upstairs to become available.

It was around 11 p.m. I was hungry, tired, and alone, and my thoughts and emotions began to decompress. I wasn't feeling self-pity. I was just upset and disappointed about what had happened. By now, the realization had set in that I would live. While lying on the side of the mountain, I hadn't been sure. Even on the helicopter and in the mobile clinic, anything could have happened to me. I could have bled internally. A broken bone could have punctured an artery inside my body. I could have gone into shock, or we might have crashed in the helicopter. Instead, I had made it here alive. That was cause for hope. The poet-king David wrote in the Psalms, "I rejoice in my broken bones." I wasn't there yet, but I was certainly rejoicing that I hadn't died.

Any potential self-pity quickly went away when the nurses brought another patient to the other side of the curtain. He was a young man. I gathered that he was in his early twenties and had broken both shoulders, both legs, and many other bones in a motorcycle accident. He was cursing and swearing, clearly very hurt and angry. Nurses tried to calm him down, but he was absolutely beside himself — and I heard everything from just a few feet away.

Compared to that guy, I really have no reason to complain, I thought. I wished I could do something for him — say something encouraging — but there was really no way to do that, given his condition and mine. Yet his presence served as a timely reminder that no matter your situation, you're always better off than someone else. It wasn't exactly an uplifting way to learn it, but it sure bumped my thoughts back to the positive side. I didn't want to sulk or rage like that guy was doing. Soon enough, the orderlies came and wheeled my bed into an elevator and to a more permanent room.

Not long after that, a face appeared at my door — Angel. How wonderful! I was medicated and tired, but it was like seeing pure sunlight. She came in with tears moistening her eyes, and when she touched me on the shoulder, it felt like life flowing into me.

After our reunion, Angel dialed Annalee on her phone and we talked about the accident and the rescue. I told her at one point, "When I was lying on the mountain all broken up, the thought did cross my mind that I didn't have to do twenty miles again tomorrow!"

She laughed. I tried not to laugh because my ribs hurt so badly when I did. The visit and the conversation were the perfect tonic for me at the end of a very challenging day, bringing healing to my mind and soul. Orderlies then gave me instructions about how to call the nurse, told me they would wake me up every four hours for medication, and that they would wake me up at six o'clock for a 7 a.m. surgery.

I was hungry. They wouldn't give me anything to eat because of the upcoming surgery. The last time I had eaten was an hour before the accident.

SURGERY

I was surprised to have a standup comedian for a surgeon.

He came in the next morning wearing a black bandanna with skulls on it! He looked like a pirate or biker, and his language and comments were appropriate for those outlaw professions. I could tell he was not a man of faith, and his whole demeanor was kind of outrageous. But I preferred a funny and genuinely nice guy to someone sour and somber in that moment.

"Here are your X-rays," he said, pulling out the slides. "Let me tell you exactly what we're accomplishing this morning. We'll do both surgeries in six or seven hours and get it all done. First, we'll put a titanium rod through your radius to attach it with screws. Your radius snapped like a pencil, so we have to pull your hand and arm apart to align the bones again. You'll be happy you're asleep for that."

I smiled and nodded, taking it in as best I could despite hunger, fatigue, and the sedating drugs coursing through my veins.

"Then we'll put four- or five-inch rods into your hip and get that solved," he continued.

It was a brief, effective presentation, and I fully understood what was about to happen. They wheeled me down to the surgery room and the next thing I knew, I was asleep and then waking up. The surgeon came in, without his black bandanna but with his cheery demeanor intact.

"I want to tell you what I told the nurses before the surgery," he said at my bedside. "I said, 'We're about to operate on a pastor, a holy man — a man of God. This is a very difficult surgery to do. We're going to pray right now and ask that God helps us because we want to make sure we take care of this man.'"

I was surprised he knew I was a pastor, and surprised at his respect for my profession. I sure didn't mind the prayers. I could only imagine what they sounded like, but in my condition, I would take anything.

"If things didn't go right with the titanium rods, we would have had to put a plate in, and that messes with your muscles and nerves," he continued. "You could have lost some function. There was a risk that your arm wouldn't work right after that. So I said, 'God, help us.'"

He looked at me for a moment as if telling an important story, then continued:

"When we put the titanium rod in and lined the bones up, the rod went right in all the way where it should be within seconds. It was a slam dunk," he finished.

Then he smiled and shook his head. I could see that what happened had impacted him.

"Prayer really works, and you're obviously good at what you do," was all I could manage to say from my hazy perspective.

He patted my shoulder softly and left, and the more I thought about it, the more my gratitude increased. Losing function in my hand would have been one of the worst outcomes, limiting my participation in activities I enjoyed most and hindering me in everyday life. God had rescued my hand function through this funny surgeon and his unexpected prayers.

I was thankful.

UP AND AT 'EM

I thought recovery would mean lying in bed for days and maybe weeks, so I was genuinely surprised the next morning when a nurse came in and said, "Hello, pastor! I attend your church. Are you ready to get up? It's time to start walking."

"What are you talking about?" I asked her. "I'm all messed up. I literally can't lift my left leg, and I don't have enough strength to get off the bed."

She was undaunted.

"We've got to get you moving right away," she said. "It's more dangerous to not move. Blood clots form, things atrophy, the twitch of the muscles stops, and the physical therapy journey takes much longer. But I'll tell you what. I'll lift your left leg for you."

My face turned hot with anger. *This is not going to work at all,* I promised myself.

She pulled my leg over the side of the bed. Of course, every inch of movement felt excruciating. I tried to baby my ribs because that's where the stabbing pain was. She then called to another nurse or orderly.

"Come over here and help me get him off this bed," she said.

Together they rotated me sideways so I was sitting up on the edge of the bed. But how was I going to stand up? As if anticipating my thoughts, the nurse fetched a walker and brought it to me.

"Put your right hand on top," she instructed. "There's a place right here, but on the left side there is a pad where you put your elbow so you don't use your forearm. Put pressure on your elbow, not your forearm."

Slowly, painfully, I stood to my unbroken leg and leaned onto the walker with the help of the second nurse. It felt ridiculous and dangerous. Thankfully, I saw they weren't going to leave me on my own. The first nurse strapped me to herself with a belt around both our waists so that if I fell, she would catch me. I felt so discombobulated that I could hardly believe I was upright.

"We're going to go the bathroom, because I know you have to go," she said.

Those were some of the most undignified moments of my life. With little, halting "steps" we finally reached the bathroom, and with the aid of the belt she helped lower me onto the toilet. Nothing was done in private, and when I was finished, I couldn't even turn around enough to wipe myself. She did it for me.

I cannot believe this is happening, I thought, trying to instantly erase it from my memory. Then, slowly, I was up again and inching back to the bed. She was nothing but encouraging and positive.

"Good job," she said. "All done. Now rest."

My day was not over. In the afternoon, the wrecking crew came back and announced, "We're going to take a little walk."

Thus began the twenty-minute process to get me out of bed. The act of rolling over took my breath away with pain.

"Put your elbow down now, Luke," my nurse gently instructed, placing my elbow on the bed. "Put your weight on your elbow. I'm going to swing your left leg around."

I am so broken. Will I ever be the same? I wondered as I pivoted.

Upright again, we inched off, strapped together, to the shower, where I suffered similar humiliations as I had that morning on the toilet. Sitting on a seat, water flowing onto me, I was helpless to bathe myself. She did it instead, efficiently and completely.

"Stand up. Let's get everywhere," she said — meaning, every crack and crevice. I somehow complied through the pain and utter humiliation. On one hand, I was thankful to be clean. On the other, I was exposed to strangers and could not get used to it. To this day when I see that nurse at church, I turn and go the other way. She has seen too much.

Back to bed I went, and the day's labors were over.

It was the same the next day, but on the third day, she shocked me with her announcement: "Okay, time to send you home. You can keep doing therapy there."

"Send me home!" I couldn't help exclaim. "I can't even get out of bed. How are you going to send me home?"

"This is your day to go home and recuperate in the comfort of your own bedroom," she reiterated.

"I'm not ready," I said. I didn't like the sound of my own words — they sounded wimpy — but I felt like a jigsaw puzzle jumbled up inside its box.

My protests prevailed, and instead of sending me home, they sent me to a room on the recovery floor for a week of full-time physical therapy to restore the use of my legs, hands, and arms. Both Angel and I were grateful for the extended care.

SUDDENLY OLD?

My body wasn't the only thing healing. My mind was as well.

Every night for the first week or so, I lay there in bed replaying what had happened. I remembered the boulder riding me down the mountainside. I went through the micro-seconds before and when it happened, recalling each movement and perception. The more I thought about it, the more I realized it was a miracle simply to be alive, and another miracle not to be in worse shape than I was. My spine and head were not affected. My body was not too badly beaten up, given the circumstances. Knowing that such a large boulder pushed me down a hardpan slope, you had to wonder, how did it miss my skull, my spine, my feet, my face? Why did it stop all of a sudden where the slope was still steep? Strangely, it gave me hope that God was in the circumstances.

Still, I had to grapple with the fact that I had really been hurt by this accident. I'm the type of person who believes that nothing bad will ever happen to me if I do my part. I had wrongly believed that if I kept my body in shape, I would be almost invincible. Suffering now was a real wakeup call to me. Life happens to everyone, including me. There is no get-out-of-all-pain pass.

I kept thinking, too, about the fact that the boulder had dislodged for me but not for hundreds of other hikers who had come by and put their hands on it. Here we were doing something for God's purposes, and the boulder came loose and chased me! I had to conclude, as Jesus had said, that it rains on the just and the unjust. I'd gotten "rained" on. Welcome to Planet Earth.

Most of those imponderables were easy enough for me to leave behind, but I was seriously concerned about how the accident would affect the rest of our lives. Would I regain normal, everyday movement? Would my hand regain dexterity? Would I ever shoot par again on the golf course? I had just shot 67 and 68 before going on the hike. Were those days over? Would I ever play basketball again? Would I ever get back on the trail with my daughter at some point? Was I facing a life of pain management, sleepless nights, and discomfort?

The most unwelcome thought was that maybe I had suddenly entered old age before my time. Would I walk with a limp the rest of my life? Would I need a walker? Could I lift things with my hands and take care of my own needs, such as grooming, dressing, and getting around the house? When you're stuck in a bed, it can feel like you'll never fully recover. I had always been optimistic about living a long, active life, and I knew from observation that accidents could put people on a new, limited trajectory. I didn't want that to happen to me.

I heard my own words echo back to me from a message I had preached called "Life Won't Wait on the Wounded." That title perhaps sounded harsh, but I had seen wounds stop people in their tracks and stunt their lives. Whatever the crisis was — loss of a child, some career setback, or maybe a relational disruption — some people responded by just stopping and getting stuck. Jesus talked about this when He said, "Let the dead bury their dead." We each have one life to live for God. Jesus wasn't being insensitive. He understood how life works. He understood that when we stop to lick our wounds, we lose time.

I didn't want that to happen to me. I made a strong decision not to let a wounded mentality slow me down. I wouldn't descend into old age before my time. I wouldn't be a burden on Angel for the rest of her life. I would lead an active life again with my kids, my grandkids, and my children-in-law. As I lay there between physical therapy sessions, I made choices about what the end result of all this would be, with God's help.

I was going to live fully, no matter what.

The more I examined the big picture, the more I felt an immense sense of gratitude. I had survived. I wasn't hopelessly crippled. Annalee was fine. I would heal up and get back to doing what I was called to do in life. In a way, the accident signaled how much the enemy hated what we were doing. The Bible says that thief comes to steal, kill, and destroy. That is his mission. He did not want young people and families rescued in our Short Creek Dream Center. He did not want girls pulled out of human sex trafficking. He didn't like the big push we were making into his realm of darkness — but he couldn't stop us, and we wouldn't stop ourselves.

We were going to finish the assignment, raise the money and awareness, and say, "To God be the glory."

THE HIKE RESUMES

My accident happened on a Saturday. My first surgery was on the next Sunday morning. True to her word, and with a whole lot of planning by our team, Annalee was back on trail on Wednesday.

Our team had regrouped and recruited a seasoned career hiker to finish the trail with her. They elected to skip the Superstition Mountains because Annalee wasn't too keen on returning to the scene of the accident. In fact, it was a hurdle for her to feel good about hiking again without me. I knew this would be the case, and Angel and I let Annalee choose when she wanted to return. She did so virtually right away, knowing that the hike was supporting so many girls and families. This wasn't about private goals anymore. It went beyond Annalee's ambitions. It was about resurrecting a town.

We were extremely careful with Annalee. The team pulled her out of the wilderness every night, pushing our vehicles to their max capacity to reach her wherever she was. Processes and people were in place to make sure she was assessed mentally and physically after what she had gone through. She ate real food and rehydrated every night.

Near Tucson, the trail required a couple of nights in the wilderness, so a good friend of ours, Troy Maxwell, went on-trail with Annalee and her hiking partner. Troy leads a thriving church in Charlotte, North Carolina, and is an expert Crossfitter. He's big, bad, and in incredible shape, but he said those two days were the hardest, most demanding of his life. I cannot thank Troy enough for being there for our family during our time of need. Not only did he step in to be a kind of dad to Annalee, but his church, Freedom House, was among the earliest monthly supporters of the work in Short Creek. In the area where he and Annalee were hiking, there was enough coyote traffic and sketchy business to make it dangerous. Angel and I were happy to have a trusted friend with her for the last few days.

HOSPITAL DAZE

Meanwhile, I was doing physical therapy and having follow-up surgeries. Angel came to visit almost every night and brought me a meal from my favorite restaurant, Houston's, so I didn't have to subsist on hospital food. She sat with me for a couple of hours each night, and we'd relax. Most of the time I fell asleep while talking to her because I was so heavily sedated.

Three times a day I went with trainers to the physical therapy gym, a rather large room with equipment such as medicine balls, elastic bands, steps and rails where you held yourself up and got your legs moving, and much more. I walked there with a walker and the nurses' help. It wasn't long before I was creeping forward on my own, without need of the safety belt that had originally held us together.

First, they wanted to figure out how much flexibility I had in my hands, especially the broken and scraped one. One simple exercise required me to put my hands palm-down on the table and raise each finger up and down repeatedly, as fast as I could.

Another exercise involved a six-inch wall and Tinker Toys.

"Reach over with your hand, grab one at a time, and put it in the bucket without dropping any," my trainer said. He timed how fast I could do twenty of them. At first I could barely pick up the toys! I fumbled around, trying to get my fingers to grasp correctly. After four or five days I completed the exercise pretty quickly and was almost back to normal. My progress encouraged me.

Then they put me between two rails to hold myself up with one hand, and placed a stair step there.

"I want to see if you can take a step up holding the rails," the therapist said.

I could step up with my right foot, but not with my left. I couldn't even move my left leg forward when walking yet.

"Can you step up on the step with the right foot, and pull your left foot up so you can stand straight?" she asked.

I was able to do that without the rails and keep my balance.

"Lift one leg in the air and balance on that leg as long as you can," she said.

I was able to do that with my right leg, and a few days later with my left leg. Progress! Every day I'd walk a little further with my walker down hospital hallways. I concentrated on using my left leg and getting it back to normal. Every day I was able to go a little further, a little faster.

Every time I got back to my room, I was tired. My body felt like it had been shaking the whole time I was using my hands and shoulders, standing on my traumatized legs, and so on. If I had listened to my body, I wouldn't have done any therapy exercises at all. That was a major learning point for me.

My left shoulder in particular was acutely painful and resisted recovery. All the skin was ripped off, and I thought I had torn my rotator cuff because I couldn't move correctly to put a shirt on. That bothered me. If I couldn't put on a shirt, how could I even think of doing normal tasks, let alone swinging a golf club or shooting a basketball?

Getting back into bed was more painful than expected, too. When I finished therapy sessions, I went through the agonizing process of simply lying down. My ribs yelped as I went horizontal. The nurse usually lowered me with a belt, swinging my left leg on the bed, while another nurse held my shoulders and back and slowly lowered me. Only when something hurt that bad did I realize how much abdominal tension and control I exercised in completing basic movements. My strategy was to do it fast, deal with the pain, and get it over with.

Seeing Angel's face at my door was the highlight of every day. I also got hundreds and hundreds of well-wishes, prayers, and encouragement from people via text. Each one provided an infusion of hope into my already-hopeful brain. Some loved ones and church members generously sent gifts, dinners, and cards. I'm not the kind of person who wants a lot of people feeling sorry for me, but I was uplifted by their concern. It was the Body of Christ in action.

There were Christians working in the hospital, too. A doctor on the floor below attended our Scottsdale campus, and he came by every day to check on me. Three of the nurses went to our church, and they brought me Nothing Bundt Cakes cupcakes! They must have been hearing from the Lord on that one.

Of course, recovery is not mostly fun, and it got old lying in a bed most of the day, sleeping because of the medications and relying on others to help me do very private things. All of that motivated me to get better faster. On my walks around the floor, I started to lap the nurses' station and they told me, "You're way ahead of what we usually see."

Nine days after I arrived, the therapists said, "You passed all your tests. You're ready to go home." Unlike the last time they proposed this, I was excited. I was able to get up and walk around the room by myself. I did it in four-inch steps, but I still did it. That morning I was able to go to the bathroom and take care of business alone for the first time, even pulling myself up from the toilet. It was indeed a great day.

I was walking around the room when Angel arrived that afternoon.

"What are you doing?" she inquired.

"I'm ready to go home!" I all but shouted.

"You are?" she said. I think she was realizing she was about to become my primary therapist!

The nurses made me use a walker to walk out of the hospital, but as soon as I got outside, I walked to the car under my own power, a nurse walking with me. Then came an unanticipated challenge.

"How on earth am I going to get into the front seat?" I asked, staring at the open passenger door on our Honda Accord.

"It'll be very tricky, Luke," the nurse replied. "Hunch down and put your butt on the seat."

I couldn't imagine doing that, so once again she slung the belt around both of us and lowered me down. Then she grabbed my left foot and swung it inside. I pulled my right foot in.

"Be careful with your right foot," she warned me. "You may be feeling good but you don't want to pull something."

I leaned back in the seat, gritting my teeth through the rib pain. The nurse closed the door and waved at us. It was good to say goodbye.

"Angel," I said as we pulled out of the parking lot, "please drive slowly and don't wreck the car."

CHAPTER 10

COMING OFF THE MOUNTAIN

It's Angel again, Luke's home therapist and wife of more than twenty-five years.

As he mentioned already, one of the first thing that disappears when you get really injured is your dignity. Modesty goes out the door. Other people are wiping your butt, showering your private parts, and emptying your pee bottle. These interactions came as quite a shock to Luke, but not for me. I had bathed and potty-trained three kids. "Mother mode" was part of my normal, and I was even happy to do my part with Luke when he got home, though I quickly learned that a guy doesn't want to be mothered by his wife. I was happy to let him figure out the toilet thing all by himself.

Because I would be his primary caretaker at home, the nurses and therapists trained me before we left the hospital. Luke would be "my patient," and I had to get comfortable with the medical tools and processes.

"Don't let him twist," they told me. "Don't let him use his arm this way. Here's how to get him up from bed. Here's how to help him lie down." I tried to take it all in and memorize the procedures that would help him heal.

No, I didn't crash the car on the way home, and as soon as we got Luke installed in the bedroom, people generously sent useful items that would help him recover. There was a raised toilet seat which proved very handy and saved the pain of hunching down. There was a recliner chair which, when activated, raised him almost to standing position. Every gesture and gift was appreciated.

Having an injured husband causes you to closely examine your whole house. If something on the floor — an object or a rug — caused him to trip, it could have had disastrous results. I walked through his pathways in advance and thought everything through to make it easier for him to live safely.

We were both on emotional journeys as well. I am not a big crier, and it takes quite a bit for me to break down. But I had a few private moments of thinking, "Everything seems to be falling apart." I don't remain in those very long, but while I was, I asked God the hard questions: "Why would You let this happen to people who were trying to raise money and awareness to rescue innocent girls from harm? Why is it so difficult to raise money in the first place? Do we have to hurt ourselves to help hurting people?"

I thought, for example, of the cowboys who put their lives in danger — one of whom got hurt — while taking water to Luke and Annalee on the trail. I thought of our team members driving four-wheelers over threatening terrains to pick up Luke and Annalee I thought of Robert the former SEAL, Ed the medic, the helicopter pilot, and others who had put their lives on the line for this cause. Many had sacrificed money, generously lending or giving equipment to us, including RVs and other vehicles. Was the price we paid too heavy for what we believed was a good cause?

On the other hand, we had chosen to do this. We accepted responsibility for making the decision to send Luke and Annalee on the trail. God had not thundered from the sky about it, though we believed His blessing was on our efforts. And it was impossible to deny that their hike had called out the goodness of people in many ways. Some had donated to the Short Creek Dream Center. Others donated toward trip costs. Some participated on our team. Some lent us their homes. God kept track of all this generosity and support, as He promised He does.

In the end, did I think it was worth it for all that, and to raise awareness and $2 million? Heck, yeah. Luke's experience would be used the rest of our lives, just his brother Matthew's seven marathons, would and his dad running from Phoenix to Los Angeles. Did we pay a price for it? Absolutely, but we had long ago chosen to squeeze everything out of life rather than floating and coasting through.

Do we pay too high a price overall? Probably not. Life is short. We want to be in that percentage of people who risk rather than choose safety. If nothing else, we are not bored. Some unfortunate souls die of boredom. If you're going Mach 2 and occasionally crashing into things, at least you're dying with style.

Normalizing

Luke had to recover mentally and emotionally from the accident as well. Some days he felt optimistic, and others he felt discouraged. Some days he felt the pain acutely, and some days it didn't seem that bad. Anger, bargaining, guilt, acceptance — I saw him cycle through them all. I was accustomed to this, as a pastor's wife. Local ministry brings you into contact with death, tragedies, and strong emotions all the time. People need someone who is not rocked and shocked, but rather mechanical who won't fan the flames of their emotions. They don't need your reactions added to theirs.

You can't speed up their process or make it go away. You're not going to successfully talk someone out of their bad day. They don't need someone nagging them and saying, "Honey, you need to be grateful. Look on the sunny side of life." The fact that we want our loved ones to get better doesn't mean we have the power to make them get better. They'll get there on their own, if you let them walk through the pain.

That said, I did find it useful to identify where Luke was in his level of healing, and attune my response to the strength of that position. If someone digs too deep into the depression, there are times to give them a fresh perspective to shake them out of it, but it has to be led by God. Ultimately, only He can minister to their spirit. Much of the time you have to let someone be mad about their situation. It's part of their grieving process. You listen and show concern, but if you rush someone past one area, you'll do more harm than good.

Luke has defied his age for years. When he set out on the hike, he was at his peak of physical ability. Lean, strong, with great stamina and a great body (since we're talking about it) — but he had lost much of that in a single moment. Imagine going from your highest capabilities to your lowest in less than ten seconds. That was the road he was walking now. Whenever he went in the direction of saying, "I'll never be the athlete I was. I'll never enjoy playing golf again," I reminded him that he had come a long way already and could not predict the future. Time would tell, and because he was a Barnett — and my husband — I had every hope of his success.

'You're No Florence Nightingale'

Meanwhile, I dropped him off at physical therapy and many doctor appointments in the weeks after he came home. Then one night, Luke's ribs hurt more than usual, and he thought maybe it wasn't his ribs at all, but that he was having kidney stones.

"The pain is across my back," he said, so I offered the cure that usually worked.

"Let's get you in the bathtub," I suggested.

"Good idea," he said.

Being in water makes a kidney stone buoyant and helps reduce the pain. We were breaking the rules a bit, because according to the nurses, baths were not allowed yet. But Luke had waterproof bandages over his stitches, and the pain wasn't subsiding, so I wheeled him in the scootable chair someone had given us. Then we encountered the tub, which was its own major obstacle. I drew the hot water and Luke lowered himself in with my help (I was thinking the belted nurse might have been useful at that time).

"This feels so good," he said. "The pain is going away."

Problem solved, I thought, feeling like Wonder Woman. But after a while, his tune changed.

"I'm too hot. I'm getting out," he announced.

I started to drain the tub and noticed he was deep down in it. The sides were slick, of course. How was I going to get him out?

"I don't think we thought this through," I said. His response was not encouraging.

"Angel, I don't feel good," he said.

I looked and saw that he had broken out in a sweat. The idea of calling 911 for help to haul him out of the tub occurred to me, but before then I thought we'd try using our combined efforts. Somehow, we got him sitting on the edge of the tub, and I carefully pivoted his legs to solid ground.

"I think I'm going to pass out," he said, and he looked it.

"Stay here. I'll get a cold towel and Gatorade," I said, leaving him on the edge of the tub to quickly grab the wheelie chair. Gingerly, we got him on it, but he was turning into dead weight as I dragged him backward across the carpet into the bedroom.

"Get me under the fan," he said. "I'm so hot."

I turned on the fan and darted out of the room for less than a minute to get ice, a towel, and an energy drink. When I returned, he was slumped back in his wheelie chair, snoring! He had clearly passed out. His eyes were rolled into the back of his head and his body was about to slide off the chair.

I killed my husband! I thought, and slapped him full-on to wake him up. He roused and his eyes opened.

"You went to sleep at a time like this?" I asked.

Then his teeth began chattering.

Good grief, I thought. *He has the chills, too?*

I grabbed my phone and called a nurse friend to try to figure out what was happening.

"His blood pressure and his blood sugars plummeted because you put him in the hot water," she said calmly. "His heart can't handle that kind of pressure, having been traumatized."

"What do I do?" I asked, growing frantic.

"Go get honey on a spoon and put it in his mouth," she said.

I did exactly as she said, and kept cooling cloths on Luke. Wouldn't you know, he perked up. As he did, I realized I'd done the opposite of everything I should have. Not to mention the creepy experience of seeing your husband lose consciousness.

"Honey, you're no Florence Nightingale," Luke said, grinning and clearly feeling better.

"I didn't sign up for this, buddy," I fumed. "This is too much responsibility for me."

"Did you take a big insurance policy out on me or something?" he joked.

At least there were no kidney stones. Maybe his ribs were healing up and reconnecting, and firing pain signals to his brain. Maybe other pains had gone away, making his rib pain stand out. I didn't know — and frankly, I didn't care. All I knew was, *No more baths!*

NORMALCY

A big part of our daily discussions involved Annalee's progress down the trail. She and the team did a great job of sending us pictures and giving us the play-by-play so we felt involved in the process. There were some really rugged days, including one where it took four hours to get our off-road vehicle to her through woods that hadn't been trimmed for fire management. Punctured tires and chainsaws were involved. It was wild.

Her journal captures her mood and mindset in those last weeks, which were up and down in more ways than one:

DAY 31 (16 MILES)

I don't know why but I was in an awful mood today. I think I'm just missing my dad. It was a beautiful day... we were hiking along the Gila River the entire time. I let my hiking partner take the lead because I wasn't feeling good.

At this point I began to cry as I hiked. I missed my dad and I felt guilty about what happened. I pulled myself together and continued on to the finish. I did a video for the church before going back to the hotel room. I talked to Kade and my mom. Shared what I was feeling. They both told me I didn't have to keep hiking — that I could stop whenever I wanted to. I told them that I couldn't do that.

DAY 32 (24 MILES)

Felt much better day. Atwood tells me my mom told him what I was feeling. He tells me he thinks I'm probably dealing with a little bit of PTSD. I don't think so. It's going to be a long day today. The hiking is through desert. Saw a MASSIVE jackrabbit. Desert skyline was gorgeous in 2nd half of the day. Stopped at our pickup point where we waited an hour for Tommy and Atwood to arrive. While we waited we met two trail angels. They gave us candy and told us they live in Oracle where they host through hikers. The man divulged his life story to me. Told me that his son had just died and that they were trying to piece their life back together. I told him about the cause and prayed with him. Sunset was picturesque.

DAY 33

Was a pretty cool day. Up and down inclines. We stopped at an old mining camp. It was abandoned and very cool. Another day of pretty desert hiking. I'm liking this section of the trail. The last 2 miles of today were uphill severely.

I'm amazed by this incredible team and humbled to be a part of this.

We had been close to our team members before, but it seemed we all grew closer during the unexpected circumstance in which we now found ourselves. Annalee had an even greater sense of mission than before. Luke was fully invested in living the experience through descriptions and photos of each day. Annalee and her hiking partners hiked three hundred miles on their own, which took close to two weeks after the interruption. It was an amazing accomplishment.

During the time when Annalee was trudging out the rest of the trail, Luke started to reengage with his normal, everyday world. When you go through a traumatic experience, for a while it's all you think about. But eventually, he wanted to get back into the office and hear how the church was doing.

There was also excitement as his physical abilities came back. Each day brought victories of some sort — less pain in a certain movement, regained function relating to doing something he loved— and I knew that my worst imaginations of how the accident would change our lives were not being realized.

I was massively thankful.

CROSSING THE FINISH LINE

Then came a surprise announcement.

"I want to finish with Annalee."

Luke's words caught me off guard, and I felt a surge of optimism with a side of, *Oh, no.* Part of me was glad he felt strong enough to try. He had undergone two surgeries, plus follow-up procedures and difficult daily therapy. He was doing well but wasn't exactly running around the block yet.

The other part of me thought, *This guy is still recovering. Can he handle any "hiking" at all? Can he even handle the four-hour drive there?*

Still, I knew that when he said he wanted to do something — like Annalee — he had pretty much made up his mind.

"Okay," I said. "What does that look like?"

"You know how we've talked about having the finish line down at Montezuma Pass by the border," he said. I did, because a hundred or so people from the church planned to go to that remote location to cheer for Annalee as she finished the AZT. Again, it was a four-and-a-half-hour drive from Phoenix — no small thing.

"I want to walk the last few hundred yards with her," he said.

I had to admit, that sounded doable — a stretch, but doable — if we approached it the right way. He felt it was important to complete the story, to cross the line together, to prove that they had overcome adversity. It would be healing for them. It would give our supporters something to cheer about. So I set about borrowing a vehicle with heavy shocks, and with the help of Luke's pain medications and a friend named Doug Hunt, who served as our driver, I took my still-healing husband way out into the wilderness to meet our daughter and finish the Arizona Trail.

Annalee, meanwhile, was finishing her dream hike.

DAY 47

It's the last day! I can't believe it. We've got only 15 miles to go. The first four are spent climbing up Huachuca Moun-tain. The view at the top is gorgeous and we stop to take pictures. I can see in all directions. We hike for a couple more miles. As we climb elevation to the last peak, we see snow!!!! Not a lot, really, just a frosting, but it's still crazy. We take our last break on the highest peak and I reflect on everything. When I come down this mountain everyone will be waiting and it will be over. It's time for us to leave and we make our descent. The going down is treacherous, and I make sure to watch my footing.

When Luke arrived at the trailhead, there was a large sign that read, "Watch out for falling rocks and boulders." Luke had the media team take a picture of him pointing at the sign. He didn't have a lot of energy to spare, so when we got there it was a matter of him walking down the trail a few hundred yards to hide behind a boulder so he could jump out and surprise Annalee and her partners.

Naturally, when they saw each other, they both were very emotional and started crying.

"I'm so proud of you," Luke told her as they embraced. "How does it feel to finish the Arizona Trail?"

"A lot better with you," she said. "It's been my dream for so long, and now it's coming to an end."

They wiped away tears and together walked toward the finish line. Our team filled the air with applause and shouts as they came into view.

Oh, God, let him not collapse, I thought as I clapped along with everyone else. I could tell this was pushing Luke's recovery, big-time. The last thing we needed were fresh injuries if he stumbled. But our best expectations won out. Annalee and Luke both spoke briefly to the gathered group, mostly about the Short Creek Dream Center and the work in Colorado City. After that, there wasn't a lot of hugging because

Luke's body couldn't handle it. He and Annalee smiled, waved, and made victory gestures all the way back to the cars, and then I drove my adventurer husband home, while Annalee rode with her fiance and his mother. Luke was content to rest his weary body and mind. That night we had dinner as a family — and with Luke's parents — for the first time since the hike began.

We all knew it was a significant achievement that meant a lot to the girls benefitting from our programs at the Short Creek Dream Center and elsewhere. Word got back to us that the girls (and the guys) were excited to see their pastor and his daughter conquer a major (and life-threatening) challenge like this. It inspired them to believe they could overcome big challenges in their own lives. All it took was the same faith and persistence Annalee and Luke had demonstrated by walking hundreds of miles.

But, in typical Barnett fashion, there was more to come — about three hundred miles more.

CHAPTER 11

A PRIVATE AFFLICTION

L uke here. As I began to recover, I went back to church and started preaching again. One day, my dad pulled me aside.

"Luke, you are preaching with a new zeal, a new passion, and more fire than ever before," he said. "It is so noticeable — like Moses when he came down the mountain and they said, 'He has been with God.' I think this was kind of a mountain experience for you."

I didn't take his words lightly. The church had continued to prosper and grow during my hike and convalescence. This fact was even more significant to us because we had taken a stand against secularist, socialist political and cultural trends in 2020 and beyond, and those stands made us controversial to some and heroic to others.

Regardless of those things, a good story is hard to hide. Large shows and media outlets like *Inside Edition*, CNN, Fox News, the *700 Club*, *Access Hollywood* and the *Arizona Republic* newspaper heard of the epic adventure and told our story. It exploded well beyond our friends and supporters to literally reach millions. Now the world was seeing what God was doing in Colorado City — and I believe that gave people hope to believe for turnarounds in their own tragic situations. Because the story had gone viral, we didn't raise a million dollars — we raised $2.4 million. We paid off all the buildings at our Colorado City facilities and had funds in hand to run the place for a couple of years. It was a major win for the families and children we served.

Everyone saw that God truly uses all things for good, for those who love Him and are called according to His purpose.

A Doctor's Story

I regularly went back for check-ups with my surgeon, and during one visit this off-the-wall, usually jolly man seemed emotional as we sat with him in his office.

"My dad passed away," he told us in a pained voice. "I don't really know a pastor, but I worked on you, and I wonder if you could help me."

"Yes," I said. I was there to receive care, but now I was the one giving it. "Would you mind if I prayed for you?"

The doctor nodded, clearly very shaken by the loss of his dad. There in his office, we laid hands on him and committed his situation to the Lord. As we did, we remembered that this doctor had prayed for me and then literally mended my wounds. Now it was our turn to pray for him in his time of distress. It was quite an amazing moment.

I also got a surprise message from the daughter of Ed, the helicopter medic, on social media. She wrote, "We were at dinner tonight and my dad said there was no way you should have survived what you did. He told our family that we need to be grateful for what we have. I want you to know we're praying for you." How cool is that? Even the medic's family was part of our prayer-support team.

Construction workers in our church looked at photos of the boulder that tried to take me out. My dad wanted to rent a helicopter, retrieve the boulder, and have it placed on the church campus as a reminder of God's protection and faithfulness. The construction guys concluded conservatively that it weighed eight thousand pounds. That's four tons! It would take a military helicopter to transport it, and would cost more than $200,000. Dad lost the vision for that when he heard the price tag!

But God was having the last word and using what happened to draw people's attention to His work. It had been His adventure from the beginning — and it wasn't over. There was a final chapter to the AZT hike, but first I had to go through something almost as painful as the injuries from that boulder. Let me explain.

SHINGLES

The accident happened in October, and I was scheduled to speak at a men's camp in North Dakota in late January. I was worried about my injuries in cold country. I had hardware in my hip and forearm and wondered how my body would react to the cold, if the rods would freeze and lock down. My body still wasn't moving very fluidly yet. I was limping along — but at least I was up and around.

I'm a private person, so I don't share things like this easily, but when I got on the plane, a very personal part of me (located in the area of my posterior) was itching and burning terribly. I had never experienced a rash or a sore so painful, especially in this particular area. The person next to me must have wondered why I was shifting back and forth in my seat for the entire flight, sometimes holding myself up on the arm rests to try to "levitate," or rotating so I was sitting almost on my hip.

I had rented what appeared to be the only car at this little airport. The itching continued as I drove to the hotel and checked in. I beelined to my room and tried to see what was happening at the affected area. It was certainly red and irritated, but I couldn't determine why.

My schedule had me preaching four times over two days at the camp. As is usual for any child of Tommy Barnett, there were many people who wanted to talk to me between sessions about how my dad's ministry had impacted their lives. Of course, there were also important times of praying with guys around the altars. I tried to ignore the pain and discomfort while I spoke and interacted with others during those full days, all the while hoping the affliction would go away. Instead, it got worse and worse.

What is going on? I kept asking myself. On the flight home, the sensation escalated into intense pain.

The next day, our church was hosting the big Kingdom Builders vision-casting meeting. I hardly slept that night. Our first service was scheduled at the Scottsdale campus. I usually get up at 5 a.m. on Sunday mornings. That day, I got up at 7:30, sweaty and with a 102-degree fever.

"Are you able to go to church?" Angel asked.

I never miss church for being sick, but this time I didn't know if I could make it. The private battle of lying there before service that morning deciding if I had the energy to go stands as one of the most epic lows of my recent days. I didn't even know if I could get up. Somehow, I got ready and showed up to church at 9 a.m. but I didn't feel like my brain was on. God miraculously moved despite what I'm sure was my poor communication. Then I drove over to the Phoenix campus, spoke again, and again God did miracles with our offering. It was remarkable to me, given how much pain I was in. Of course, God's power has never had anything to do with my "performance," anyway.

By the time I made it back to the house, nothing had improved. I had no idea what the problem was, and the next day Angel and I went to the emergency room. A nice young doctor came in and promptly informed me what was inflaming the most private regions of my body.

"You've got shingles, and you've got it in a very rough spot," he said. "It's common among men over fifty who have had a traumatic experience. I believe it was caused by the stress of your accident."

He prescribed medication and said optimistically that it would be gone in a maximum of six weeks. For me, it lasted eleven or twelve weeks and would not go away. All the while, I was recovering from my injuries and going to physical therapy.

We have a saying around the church that comes from my dad and is part of our culture: "Don't call in, crawl in." We aim to be tough. If one of us is sick, we don't have to stay home; we crawl into the office and get our work done. I have watched my dad do that all these years. The way he put it, the cause is more important than how we feel, and the most important thing in the world is the work of the Lord. We are servants of the Lord. We don't get to just quit or take a day off.

During those truly awful, itchy weeks, I would get up each morning and go to work, and I didn't tell anyone what I was feeling. I remembered what our family friend, football player and coach Denny Duron, told me one time: "When I'm down or hurting or depressed, people don't care. You have to learn to play well, hurt. It's not just about staying in the game, it's about rising above. Part of that is playing so well that no one knows you're hurting."

That's why only a few close friends and family members knew about my case of shingles. In all honesty, people in staff meetings and at church didn't want to know. They wanted their leader to be an encourager. They wanted me to rise above it.

Easter fell within that eleven-week period, and at our Good Friday service I found myself at my wits' end. I got up in front of a couple of thousand people at our outdoor amphitheater and preached on the weight of the cross. In so many ways I was talking to myself. Shingles was a small thing compared to what some people go through, but compared to the accident, the surgeries, and the physical therapy, shingles in some ways felt worse — and lasted longer.

People sometimes think I live a perfect life, but this was a low point for me and really the only time I questioned God in that season. I walked off the platform that night feeling totally spent and even a bit angry about what I was suffering. Having played hurt for nearly three months, I felt like throwing in the towel. I wondered how much more I could take and if I would ever get back on top of things. Normally, I would have stayed after the service and shaken every last hand, but tonight was different. I made a direct line for my car. I just wanted to get away from everyone.

But standing there waiting for me offstage was my good friend, Doug Hunt. To my surprise, he was crying.

"That … was the most amazing message I've ever heard!" he said in his distinctive, enthusiastic way. "That changed my life tonight."

Doug is the ultimate encourager and people person. He's six-foot-four or -five, tall and skinny. He is larger than life and has a zest for living. He also has tremendous interpersonal skills. He never wants to talk about himself, but wants to listen to what's going on in everyone else's life.

Doug had no idea what I was going through physically, but his words melted me. The message I had just preached felt like the worst I'd ever given. To see its effect on him was profound for me.

Doug peered at me. He could tell something was off.

"Are you okay?" he asked.

Very uncharacteristically, I responded, "No." I can't remember giving that answer to anyone before. I always say, "I'm doing great." Barnetts are "tomorrow is going to be better than today" people. But I had reached a place of physical vulnerability. The shingles were attacking my nerves. I was taking pills and applying topical medications. The affliction was creating deep scars which almost look like ruts, which I still bear in my body.

Doug stared at me, shocked, because he'd never heard me give a negative reply. Three years before that, he had been in a dirt-biking accident: He'd hit a deer, flipped over his handlebars, and snapped multiple ribs and a collarbone. Dad and I were the first to show up to visit him at the hospital. He had wept as we'd prayed for him.

Now, years later, he was seeing me in my own broken state. Somehow his prior vulnerability, and even his words that night, opened up a flow of vulnerability from me. I told him I had shingles. I told him life had virtually ceased for me as I'd barely been able to leave the house because of my combined afflictions. At the same time, all our people were taking blows from those in the secular culture because President Trump had visited our church that summer, and were standing up against abortion, assaults on the biblical identity of men and women, and more. We were one of the churches leading the charge on a raft of issues, hosting monthly Freedom Nights in America and bringing in the best conservative and Christian speakers. I wanted to embolden pastors not only to be people of compassion but also to stand for the whole counsel of God. I believe the devil tried to kill me, thinking that if he could get rid of me, it would help his wicked cause.

I'm sure I said some of this to Doug, but what I remember most is when he opened his arms and embraced me.

"You're going to get through this," he said. "We are with you."

Then he did the most powerful thing: He laid hands on me and prayed an amazing prayer. He declared by faith that I would be well. He did not weakly ask for God's will to be done — no, he declared that God's will was to heal, and he thanked God in advance for what He would do with the rest of my life. By then, I was crying with him. Instead of crawling out of that service, I flew out of there. Doug's response strengthened me. I had confided in someone I truly respected, and now he was in my corner, fighting with me. It felt awesome.

Shortly after that, I started to heal up. The shingles went away, leaving their telltale scars. Not many days later, I played golf and shot 67, which is 5 under par — a stellar day on the links. I credit the faith in Doug's prayer and God's response for the acceleration of my healing.

As relieved as I felt, the aches and pains of my injuries didn't fully go away for a year and a half. Taking a wrong step made my hip twinge. My forearm took the longest to heal, having suffered a severe break. The rod in my bone felt like it was pushing down on my wrist, putting pressure on all the little bones. After seven or eight months, that discomfort finally went away. I never had real problems with my hip. Three long screws are in there. I feared walking with a limp, but that went away and soon enough I could walk normally.

When Annalee got married in January 2021, a couple of months after the accident. I was happy to be well enough to walk her down the aisle.

FINISHING THE AZT

I didn't give a lot of thought to finishing the hike until early 2022, when I felt completely well. I was writing a book about the experience but didn't feel good about how the story was ending. I wanted to complete the hike, and the story of it would have to end in a better way than just meeting Annalee at the end of her own trail journey. So one day I said measuredly and with considered certainty, "Angel, I want to finish the Arizona Trail."

"Are you sure you want to do that?" she responded, naturally. "It's still three hundred miles."

But she knows me well enough to realize she wasn't going to talk me out of it. I think my recovery had surprised all of us, and so she got behind the effort and even determined to raise more money for the Short Creek Dream Center as a way of beating the devil with his own stick.

I am thankful that the final three hundred miles were less eventful than the first five hundred. Again, I trained to get ready for the relentless up-and-down days. I decided to start at the southern extreme, on the border of Mexico, and work my way up to the boulder, the site of the accident.

Two great guys, Josh Ursue and Andy Shipe, became my initial trail partners. They both attend the Dream City Church Scottsdale campus. Andy is an absolute beast and a military veteran, which was important for us down by the border where things can get lawless. Josh is a lifetime hiker who has trekked the Swiss Alps and all the major U.S. trails. Later on, Jason Fronstien, a bank owner in our church, blessed me by taking two weeks off and to serve as my hiking partner. He trained his heart out and was in such great shape. All three guys were a pleasure to be with.

I'm not sure they could always say the same of me. I had trained for distance but not for elevation, and the first day, which took us up the eleven-thousand-foot Miller Peak, laid that fact bare. I was crawling up the trail as Josh and Andy left me in the dust. My lungs were on fire and my body locked down with dehydration. I barely made it to the campground. The guys had brought all kinds of supplements and used them to nurse me back to health. We camped that night near the top of that mountain, eating MREs. We talked about the sobering sights we'd witnessed down on the border: debris — mostly clothing — left by groups of illegal immigrants, and actual people crossing the border looking uncertain and a little sheepish. The camaraderie and rest that night totally rejuvenated me.

The next morning, we enjoyed an eighteen-mile hike, all downhill from nine thousand feet. The heat rose and the terrain changed back to high desert. That was my only experience with cramping and muscle fatigue. From there I became stronger than I had been even on the earlier portion. By the end, I was running up trails.

I had gone into that section of the hike with concerns about how twenty miles a day would affect my new hardware. With four pins in my hip and a rod in my arm, would everything hold up? Would complications arise? Would the metal shift around or start settling wrongly? To my great relief, those concerns did not materialize and soon I simply forgot to be concerned. I just enjoyed the rolling, up-and-down terrain of southern Arizona and the fellowship of my companions.

The final three hundred miles took us three weeks. Each Friday, I came back to Phoenix and preached two church services, one at Scottsdale and one at our main campus. On Sunday afternoons I would drive back to the trailhead to start the hike again on Monday morning. The memories are plenty: hiking in sleet and cresting a mountaintop where Jason and I saw a huge albino deer; following the trail through several private ranches, which included walking through herds of cattle (with whom we took pictures); enjoying hours of conversation with Jason, Josh, and Andy, who are just wonderful guys; having the pleasure of Joe and Dave Ansell, our Scottsdale campus pastors, joining us for a couple of days. (Joe got awful blisters on his feet, so we nicknamed him Tenderfoot; Dave became the Lost Boy because he got lost while training for the hike — everyone earns a trail name).

The hike wasn't easy, but we had so much fun together, laughing, sharing deeply, and living life in that beautiful setting, that I was also able to forge memories on top of what Annalee and I had already experienced. My daughter was also coaching me from afar and was especially excited for me to experience her favorite hotel in Patagonia, where a famous racehorse named Secretariat had been kept at one point. The place was part hiker, part biker, and full of rustic charm. We stayed there two nights.

Meanwhile, Angel was raising more money just to kick the devil in the teeth and bring glory to God. "I'm just your mule," I told her at one point. "You just use me to raise money." I guess we both have a weird sense of humor.

BACK AT THE BOULDER

Through it all, I knew I was approaching the end of the hike and returning to the place where I could have lost my life.

We had thought this part through. Angel was going to join me on the trail for that last portion and hike seven miles in with me to the boulder. Then she and I would turn around and hike seven miles out via the same trail we had taken in. Angel had trained with me on Elephant Trail before. She's a gamer with a strong disposition; I knew she wouldn't have any trouble, and she didn't. We got up at 5 a.m. that last morning, and a friend drove us into the Superstition Mountains to the location where Jason and I had left off the night before. It was rough territory and slow going to get there, but we finally made it. Then Angel and I donned orange hats and draped big red flags on our hiking poles because it was deer season and we'd heard gunshots everywhere (a fact that greatly concerned some members of our church, but again, God protected us).

This was new trail to me, and as usual we started the hike talking, then quieted down after a while and put in headphones, settling into a groove. After a couple of hours, I spotted a big, dry wash with a trail zig-zagging down its face.

"We're getting close," I told Angel.

It felt quite somber, knowing I would come face-to-face with the massive rock that had almost killed me. As we got closer, the scene looked more and more familiar. I saw the steep area from which the boulder had been dislodged. To me it appeared much steeper now, almost vertical, which explained why it continued to slide for so long. I proceeded up the trail to where I had told Annalee, "Careful, it's getting steep here." As Angel and I were reflecting quietly, suddenly Annalee herself jumped out from behind a bush, now seven months pregnant and smiling broadly.

"Annalee! What?!" I said.

Anytime I see Annalee, I feel so much joy in my heart. She is the sweetest, kindest person, and such a loyal friend. I started laughing, even crying tears of joy because here we were, finishing together again, and so unexpectedly.

"How did you get here? Did you stay overnight?" I asked her, bewildered.

She told me that generous people in our church had dropped her off a mile away in a helicopter, and she had hiked to the accident site with two guys who carried video equipment so they could record the (for me) unanticipated reunion. We laughed about how she had gotten a doctor's permission to do this even though she was bigger than a house, and the fact that she still had her trail legs while the media guys were huffing and puffing behind her.

We turned to the place where the accident had happened. Neither of us could believe how big the boulder was, but what really shocked me was how it had stopped. There was one small boulder the size of a football upon which it rested, which apparently had stopped its momentum. When I saw how small the rock was that was holding it in place, I was struck by the sheer miracle of what had happened.

I recalled the Tuesday night meeting at the Prayer Pavilion when a man had walked up to Pastor Said and said, "I had this vision last night of something attacking Pastor Luke, and an angel was holding back the force that was trying to kill him." I believed it. I also was even more convinced that it had been an attack from the enemy, but a failed one.

I've never been a spooky person about spiritual things. I'm on the practical side of Christianity. I don't see demons wherever I go; I see God wherever I go. But I do believe that in 2020 and beyond, we were helping to start a new movement among churches to stand against moral decay in our culture. I truly believe the devil wanted to take us out right there, and that God stopped the attempt and used it for good by publicizing our church's efforts to rescue human trafficking victims, which was what the hike was all about. I didn't like the fact that I got hurt, but it caused millions of people to hear positive things about Dream City Church at a time when we could have been swamped by negative publicity — and if that was God's plan, then it was well worth it to me. God gave the enemy the back of His hand by giving us the front page of the papers.

The Bible says God will prepare a table for you in the presence of your enemies. Looking at that boulder, I knew I was seeing His faithfulness in real time.

Annalee had had a small placard made to place near the site, to commemorate God's intervention. We nailed that placard and stake into the ground so other hikers would see it and read about the miracle when they passed by. Then we walked higher and saw where the big rock had been dislodged, and I slowly made my way down that section of trail. I have to admit that a little PTSD hit me. My thoughts went back to what I was thinking when the rock began to slide.

This is going to kill Annalee. Just get her out of the way.

I saw the spot where I had shoved her. Then came my second thought: *This is not real. Things like this don't happen to me.*

Then it was, *I feel my bones breaking. It's only a matter of time until it hits my head, and that'll be the end. The lights will go out.*

I remembered when the boulder spat me out a little and I had screamed, "Get me out of here!" I remembered feeling frantic and thinking I was moments from death. I remembered Annalee grabbing my straps and pulling me to safety, all business and using her training.

"Can you feel your toes?" I remember her asking. "Can you bend your leg? Are you having trouble breathing?"

I remembered sending her off to try to get a signal with the satellite phone, assuring her that I wouldn't die of internal bleeding. I remembered the world going black and white. I remembered Annalee returning. I remembered the tremendous peace I had about whether I lived or died. I knew I loved the Lord and He loved me, and nothing would separate me from His love — not even a crushing boulder.

Now I sat down and stared at the four-ton slab for a while, and the small rock holding it up. The reality of the miracle hit me repeatedly. This wasn't just fate, chance, or luck. It was the providence of God.

We stayed there forty-five minutes or so, taking photos and videos and hanging out to remember. It didn't feel like a place of doom but a place of victory and remembrance. A lot of times those caves and valleys, the places that look like death, turn out to be the greatest places because God is there. David met God in caves. We find out who we are in the caves of life. We don't like them, but it's usually where we meet God in the most impactful way. I had preached these things for years, but at this spot I had lived it.

I still couldn't figure out how Annalee would hike out pregnant until we made our way up the steep hill and I saw a helicopter's rotors turning. I felt like saying, "Hallelujah! I'm done with the trail." I was so glad I didn't have to hike out!

They flew us from the boulder back to a hangar at an air park. For the first time I sensed a feeling of complete closure: We had accomplished what we had set out to do. The hike was finally over.

Just then, the hangar door opened and 150 people from our church shouted, "Surprise!" A beautiful scene lay before us — tables set up, music from a live band, a barbecue ready to be served. The people hugged us and shook our hands. I haven't experienced too many storybook endings, but this certainly was one, and it was all Angel's doing. She wanted to bless me, so she and her friend Annette Carlson (and her husband, Tim) planned this amazing event.

At last, Annalee and I had finished our dream of hiking the Arizona Trail — and used it to do a lot of good for young victims in Arizona. It was a story of restoration, healing, and love — and of God's protection for us all against things that could have taken our lives, but didn't.

EPILOGUE

They say there's the journey you intend, and there's the journey you take. That was certainly the case for me and Annalee. But it was also the case for our cause. Since we set out on our hike, the Short Creek Dream Center has received not $1 million but $3.4 million in donations — and climbing. Clearly, God is funding the work there as people learn of what's happening. He is even using this book to accomplish that goal.

As I write this, it has been three years since the boulder chased me downhill, and I have fully recovered. I walk normally, I play golf, and I have no limitations to my daily routine. I am thankful.

I am also thankful for the lessons learned in the furnace of that experience. All adventures unsettle our norms, make us uncomfortable, and cause us to grow. We can't know everything that will happen, and I am more convinced than ever that we must embrace healthy risks to reap any rewards. It doesn't mean launching out on a life-defining hike the way I did, but it may feel dangerous anyway. Changing a job, starting a school or a business, moving to another state, pioneering a church, getting married, having a family — all of these are risks we take with huge potential upsides. Each of them could go wrong, but we do them for the promise of what might go right.

You have to lean into the mountain. That was the phrase Angel used when teaching me to ski when we were dating.

"Remember to lean forward and attack the mountain," she said. "The tendency is to lean back because of fear."

That's good life advice, too. Lean into the direction you want to go, even if it speeds up and scares you. Every time you do, you increase your faith that with God, all things really are possible.

Will you crash sometimes? Sure, you will. But the truth is, even this book is a lot more interesting because of the crazy things that happened to us and not some bland account of our triumphs. People want to hear about danger averted, pain overcome. We want to be on the edge of our seats, wondering how someone survived and how they got out of each mess.

Ultimately, an adventure isn't something you read about, it's something you do. Internet videos of cool adventures won't cut it — and neither will this book. It's time to take an adventure of your own. I find that when you head out on a true adventure:

— you pray harder
— you work harder
— you feel more alive
— you develop quicker thinking
— you gain faster reaction time
— you create solutions
— you feel exhilarated in the face of events
— you laugh deeper and harder
— you serve with more gusto
— you give more away

— you climb higher mountains

— you run longer races

— you make more money (it's biblical!)

— you deepen relationships with others

— you truly live life.

If it's been a long time since you felt your heart pound and your mind race, it's possible you're in a place of devastating safety. Nobody gets to the end of a safe, comfortable life, looks back and says, "Those were great memories."

So the question is, "What adventure is God asking you to take?"

Maybe it involves a relational risk.

Maybe it involves a new vocation.

Maybe it involves bold generosity.

Maybe it involves moving more into ministry.

Of course you're going to be afraid. That's the nature of it. When we make ourselves available for something new, we might discover our passion lies in new areas. Are you open to having your purpose and your passion redirected? Are you open to life being different — and better?

Let me point out a few common personality traits that keep people from moving forward. The first is The Perfectionist. If this is you, you don't want to start a task unless you're able to do it in a way that meets impossibly high standards. You put off starting anything until conditions are perfect — and of course they're never going to be perfect, so you never start!

Ecclesiastes 11:4 (TLB) counsels, "If you wait for perfect conditions, you will never get anything done." Perfectionists are not doers; they are excuse makers. Don't be that guy or that girl.

The second personality is The Dreamer. Dreamers keep things vague, general, and grandiose. They hate particulars and choose to ignore them. Because adventures involve details, they never go on one. Their mouths speak of big plans, but their minds and hands never get down to the work. Dreamers sound good but produce nothing.

The third personality type is The Paralyzed. People who become physically paralyzed cannot feel certain parts of their body. They are numb. Many people feel numb in their hearts because it's been so long since they had an adventure. They neither laugh nor weep with any conviction. Some of you may be suffering from dream leakage, like a balloon slowly losing its helium. You may feel emotionally or mentally droopy, or you may feel nothing at all. Your zip zipped away somehow.

The psalmist often wrote about his heart being dry, and of being in a dry and weary land. It's a bad condition to fall into. Adventure refreshes us and brings life back to our minds and bodies. It removes paralysis and numbness.

The last personality type is The Wounded. In my freshman year of high school, I decided to try out for the wrestling team. We had a guy on our team named Mark. He was the state champion as a freshman and sophomore, and he never lost a match in his first two seasons of high school wrestling. College recruiters showed up to watch Mark wrestle. The crowd would roar as he effortlessly pinned his opponents in a matter of seconds. His talent allowed him to have big dreams, even of the Olympics.

The following year, we got a new wrestling coach named Coach Carlson. He was tough in his own way, and it didn't take long for him to notice a tragic flaw in Mark's character: attitude One day as we spread out to do pushups, Mark didn't drop down with the rest of us.

"Get back on the mat and do pushups like everybody else," Coach Carlson said, and Mark flared up at him.

That was the first of many flare-ups. Because of Mark's God-given ability, he was easily able to win the starting position in his weight class, and as the season began, college scouts showed up at his matches. He was the big deal at our school and people talked about how he would be able to write his own ticket to any university.

But after multiple flare-ups, the day came when Coach Carlson saw that Mark's defiance was damaging the morale of the entire team. Coach sat his best wrestler on the bench.

By this time, I had gotten to know Mark and discovered that his father was abusive toward him. This caused Mark to react badly whenever someone told him what to do. He was wounded, but that wound threatened his athletic career.

The day after Mark was benched, he showed up at practice.

"I quit," he announced.

Coach Carlson replied, "Fine, Mark, go ahead and quit. You'll quit wrestling today and someday you'll get married and quit that. One day you'll get a job and quit that. Go ahead and quit, Mark, and you'll be a quitter the rest of your life."

I think Coach could have handled him better, but that was the way it went. Mark quit wrestling. Eight years later, I played in a golf tournament with Mark's dad, and he told me that Mark was doing well and that he and Mark had reconciled. I was glad to hear that — but the future Mark had dreamed of was already gone. When he quit the team, college scouts quit calling. Olympic gold slipped beyond the horizon. His wrestling talent got him nowhere.

Mark is a good example to me that life won't wait on the wounded.

If we wallow around and take our time getting over hurts, life moves on without us. Unfair though it may seem, opportunities pass us by when we spend time being wounded. This is why Jesus told people who wanted to follow Him, but had reasons to delay, to get their priorities in line. (See Luke 9.) The hurts and failures of yesterday will do nothing to help you reach your tomorrows. The Wounded miss out on life if they wait until they are healed to proceed. Being wounded becomes an effective trap.

God never promised any of us that if we follow Him, our lives will be easy. You might get hurt once or twice. You might narrowly avoid death like I did. Maybe you already have. But did you know that God has removed eternity from the equation? The Bible promises, nothing can separate you from the love of God which is in Christ Jesus. Not life nor death nor anything else. (See Romans 8:39.) God has removed all eternal risk for His followers. That means we can take all kinds of risks here on Earth, knowing that ultimately we have life and the love of God forever. We can never lose it.

If you don't have enough faith to finish a new adventure, just have enough faith to start one. That's all it takes. When I first preached a sermon, I couldn't have fathomed that I would speak every week to thousands. I only had faith to do it that one time. God gives us power along the way. He meets us in the fire. That is His promise to you and to me.

I've never started a ministry endeavor with the money or manpower to finish. My dad taught us that money follows ministry. When you start the adventure, the windows of provision open up and fuel your efforts. Power comes along the way.

The truth is that life follows vision. Where is your vision today? Are you on an adventure, or are you feeling paralyzed, wounded, stuck in perfectionism, maybe procrastinating? What's in the way of you starting?

When's the last time you looked up and dreamed — and then did something to make that dream come true?

If what we're doing at Short Creek Dream Center, and what Annalee and I learned on the trail of our epic trip, has any value, I hope it's to spur you to a new season of adventure in your life. Adventure is the natural result when God guides your steps.

He makes everything good — even the painful moments — when you choose to adventure your life.